Skyquake

Also available in this series:

Selected Poems

Adam / Adán
Square Horizon / Horizon carré
Equatorial & other poems / Ecuatorial y otros poemas
Arctic Poems / Poemas árticos
Painted Poems *
Paris 1925: Ordinary Autumn & All of a Sudden / Automne régulier & Tout à coup
Skyquake / Temblor de cielo
Altazor *
Citizen of Oblivion / El ciudadano del olvido
Seeing and Touching / Ver y palpar
Last Poems / Últimos poemas
Uncollected Poems / Poemas inéditos *

Manifestos / Manifestes
Adverse Winds / Vientos contrarios

El Cid / Mío Cid Campeador
Cagliostro
Three Huge Novels / Tres inmensas novelas (with Hans Arp)
Papa, or The Diary of Alicia Mir / Papá, o el diario de Alicia Mir *
Satyr, or The Power of Words / Sátiro, o el poder de las palabras

Volodia Teitelboim: *Vicente Huidobro — in perpetual motion. A Biography*

* not yet published at the time the current volume was released

Vicente Huidobro

Temblor de cielo
Skyquake
Tremblement de ciel

Translated from Spanish & French by
Tony Frazer

Shearsman Books

This second, expanded and revised edition
published in the United Kingdom in 2025 by
Shearsman Books Ltd
PO Box 4239
Swindon SN3 9FN

Shearsman Books Ltd Registered Office
30–31 St. James Place, Mangotsfield, Bristol BS16 9JB
(this address not for correspondence)

www.shearsman.com

EU AUTHORISED REPRESENTATIVE:
Lightning Source France
1 Av. Johannes Gutenberg, 78310 Maurepas, France
Email: compliance@lightningsource.fr

ISBN 978-1-84861-979-1

Translations, Notes and Introduction copyright © Tony Frazer, 2006, 2019, 2025.

The right of Tony Frazer to be identified as the translator of this work has been asserted by him in accordance with the Copyrights, Designs and Patents Act of 1988. All rights reserved.

Temblor de cielo was originally published in Madrid in 1931 by Editorial Plutarco S.A. The French version, *Tremblement de ciel*, first appeared in Paris in 1932, published by Éditions de l'As de Cœur. The first Chilean edition, with some revisions, appeared in Santiago from Editorial Cruz del Sur in 1942. The Spanish text here follows the 1942 edition.

This translation was first issued in an earlier form, with only the Spanish text and a translation thereof, by Shearsman Books in 2019. This second edition of the book features a large number of textual revisions to the translation of the Spanish text, and minor amendments to the Introduction. The French text, and *its* translation, appear here for the first time.

A first version of the translation of the Spanish text was published as *Sky Tremor* in the online magazine, *Fascicle*, in 2006. Thanks to Tony Tost, editor of *Fascicle*, and the late Kent Johnson for their encouragement at that time. The text benefited from close readings and suggestions from René de Costa, doyen of Huidobro scholars, and Mark Weiss, which prevented several embarrassing errors. This final publication also benefited from some suggestions by Valentino Gianuzzi, for which I am most grateful. Any errors that remain are of course strictly the fault of the translator.

CONTENTS

Portrait of Vicente Huidobro by Hans Arp   6

Introduction   7

12   Temblor de cielo / Skyquake   13

70   Skyquake / Tremblement de ciel   71

Notes   129

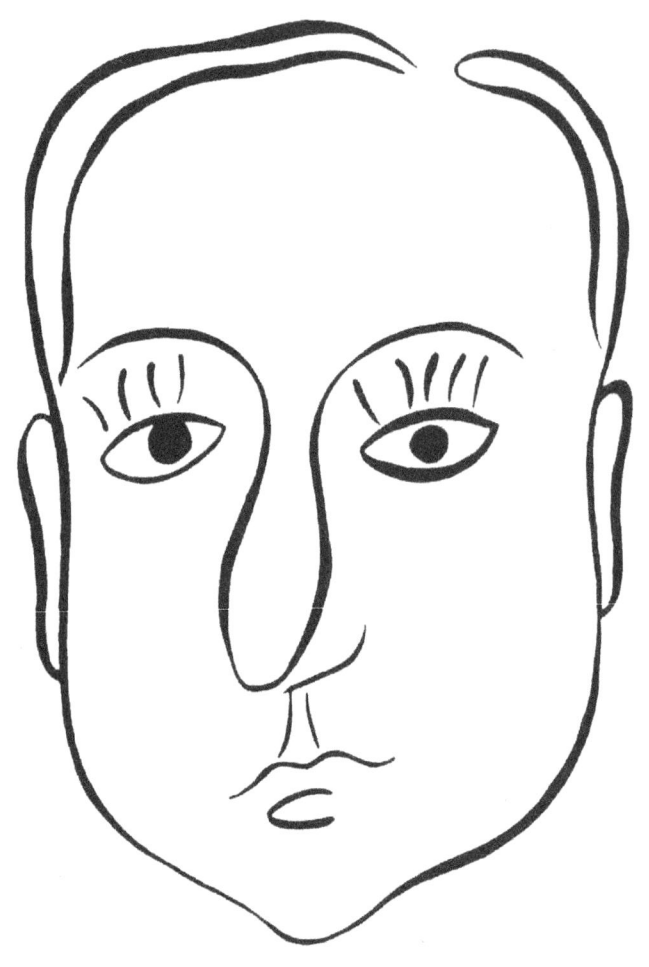

Portrait of Huidobro by Hans Arp, Paris, 1931.

Vicente Huidobro and *Temblor de cielo*

The Chilean poet Vicente Huidobro (1893–1948) is one of the most important figures in 20th-century Hispanic poetry and, along with César Vallejo, one of the pioneering avant-gardists in Spanish literature. Like Vallejo, he lived for many years in Paris but, unlike his Peruvian contemporary, he participated fully in the city's various artistic movements. Influenced initially by Apollinaire, whom he met within weeks of arriving in the city, Huidobro fell in early with forward-looking French writers such as Apollinaire, Reverdy, Cocteau and Cendrars, as well as with the expatriate Spanish artists' colony, which included Picasso and Juan Gris.

Originally from an upper-class Santiago family, Huidobro was fortunate to have the means to support himself and his family while he found his artistic way, and—after an early phase in his native country writing in a quasi-symbolist style, influenced by Rubén Darío—he threw himself into the Parisian artistic milieu with a passion, quickly becoming a notable figure. He also wrote in French, sometimes translating his own works into French, sometimes composing in both languages. His early forays in French were somewhat uncertain and the manuscripts show handwritten interventions by the poet Pierre Reverdy and the artists Francis Picabia and Juan Gris, among others. It would seem that some of the early French poems were in fact largely translated by these friends.

Octavio Paz referred to Huidobro as *el oxígeno invisible* (the invisible oxygen) of Latin American poetry, reflecting the fact that his influence was felt by poets right across the continent; in fact he was probably *the* major link between the European avant-garde and progressive literary circles in Latin America.

He was a also a successful novelist: *Mío Cid Campeador*—published in English translation in 1931 as *Portrait of a Paladin*—created a stir, and his screenplay-turned-into-a-novella *Cagliostro*—also published in English in 1931 as *The Mirror of a Mage*—won a $10,000 prize from the League for Better Motion Pictures as the best candidate for movie adaptation, but was never made into a film, because of the arrival of the *talkies* shortly afterwards.[1] Then too, he was an inveterate polemicist—a writer of artistic manifestos and founder of the Creationism movement (*Creacionismo*), a

---

[1] New editions of these translations were issued in this series by Shearsman Books in 2019, as *El Cid* and *Cagliostro*, respectively.

politician (sometime member of the Communist Party, he also ran for the Presidency of Chile as leader of the Youth Party), and a journalist, including a stint as a foreign correspondent during World War 2.

Huidobro was a restless soul and an artist of the very highest calibre. Today he is probably most revered for his extraordinary long poem *Altazor*, written, according to the author, over a period of some 12 years and finally published in 1931. (It should be said here that it is actually more likely that the poem was composed over a period 4 or 5 years, perhaps building on a shorter piece from the period after the 1918 poem, *Ecuatorial*. The manuscript evidence is unclear.) Less well-known is the long prose poem *Temblor de cielo*, also published in 1931 and mostly written in 1928. Huidobro regarded the two works as the summation of his work up to that point.

Altazor is the archetypal modernist Big Poem and belongs with other titanic efforts such as *The Waste Land* and *Trilce*. It is fragmentary and alludes to the glories of the future, symbolised by flight, but also shows language breaking down under the onslaught of the new. The prose-poem *Temblor* is more apparently unified, although this might owe more to its style of delivery, as well as its rapid composition: an ecstatic outpouring of words that largely revolve around the themes of love, sex and death. The Isolde to whom much of the poem is addressed is an idealised feminine figure—part goddess, part idealised beloved, part Isolde from Wagner's opera (another ecstatic outpouring on the themes of love, sex and death) and part Ximena Amunátegui, the young woman who had become the poet's second, albeit common-law wife (her status was due to the fact that Vicente remained legally married to Manuela Portales, the mother of his four children).

I tend to suspect that the central impetus for the work is an erotic storm driven by the author's new marital situation, notwithstanding the artistic fusion with the other elements mentioned above. The poem is also a sustained lyric effusion of a kind that Huidobro had never produced before, and it marks the point at which his work moves on from the barnstorming avant-garderie of his younger years to a more mature style, albeit one heavily influenced by surrealism, a movement which Huidobro had previously attacked. It is also the last time that Huidobro was to adopt the god-like narrative persona that occurs in his earlier work. In *Temblor*, as in some earlier works, God is conflated with the poet-creator, as he is in *Altazor*, where the opening lines reflect the opening of a love-poem to Ximena that the author published (to great scandal, in 1926) in the Santiago newspaper, *La Nación*:

Nací a los treinta y tres años, el día de la muerte de Cristo
[I was born at the age of thirty three, on the day Christ died].

(By way of clarification, it should be noted that the author was 33, the supposed age of Christ at the time of *His* death, when he first met Ximena, which gives the imagery another dimension.)

Temblor de cielo exists in two versions, one in Spanish and one in French. There is doubt over which version has primacy, although it has been argued that the French version precedes the Spanish, if not throughout its entire composition. As there are no extant manuscripts, it is unlikely that we will ever know the truth of the matter. In this second edition of *Skyquake*, we are reissuing the translation together with *both* the Spanish and the French texts of the poem. There are a number of differences between the two texts, but little in the way of major discrepancies, and some of those may well be the result of transcription errors, or typesetting errors.[2] The texts have been set so that those who wish to see the Spanish opposite the French can do so, albeit by holding a number pages up to permit an almost *en-face* arrangement. The texts used are those versions published in the author's *Obra poética* (Poetic Works, ed. Cedomil Goic. Paris: Ed. ALLCA XX, 2003), which adopts some later revisions by the author, but we have corrected some minor typographical errors here and there, especially in the French version.

The translation of the title requires some explanation: in Spanish, a *temblor* is an earthquake, albeit less severe than a *terremoto*, more of a tremor, a shaking perhaps; one would expect differing words for gradations of an event that occurs regularly in a seismic zone such as Chile and, indeed, when I was resident there, I always heard the frequent *small* earthquakes referred to as *temblores*. Hence, one valid translation of the title could be *Sky Tremor*—and that was my title when the first version of this translation was published. The French title is *Tremblement de ciel*, on the surface cognate with the Spanish, but 'earthquake' in French is *tremblement de terre*, even though *tremblement* on its own would usually be translated as "tremor". Given this, and also the massive quake which occurs in the poem itself, I

---

[2] To give one example: near the end of the piece (pp. 68/69), there is a phrase "eyes closed" (*ojos cubiertos*, lit. "eyes covered") in the Spanish, whereas the French (pp. 126/127) has *yeux ouverts* ("eyes open"). I tend to think that the French should read *couverts* ("covered" / "closed"), in line with the Spanish, but have no documentary evidence to support this position, and have thus left the text as it is.

have now opted for *Skyquake* as being the preferable translation. Neither version is absolutely correct: I suggest that the reader chooses the one s/he prefers. There is a further wrinkle to this little mystery: Óscar Hahn has suggested that the poem was actually begun in French,[3] with a French title, and that the slightly odd Spanish title—grammatically, it should be *Temblor <u>del</u> cielo*—is in fact a back-translation from the French.

For those chiefly interested in the original Spanish text, with full introduction and critical apparatus, there is a good, and cheap, reading version from Cátedra in Madrid, coupled with *Altazor*, edited by René de Costa. The French version can be had in the Goic edition of the *Obra poética* referred to above—this is by far the best edition of Huidobro's poetry available, although it is expensive and no longer easy to find. There is also a separate edition in France: *Tremblement de ciel*, Paris: Editions Indigo & Côté-femmes, 2008, which I have not seen, and it is not even clear to me that the book is still in print, or whether the press still exists—it specialised in Latin American poetry in French translation.

§ § §

As mentioned above, this second edition of *Skyquake* amplifies the first edition of 2019, which was the first Huidobro volume planned for the Shearsman list, but which was rapidly joined by others, initially *Arctic Poems* and *Square Horizon*, but subsequently all the mature poetry—this process is still incomplete as we go to press—and several prose volumes. The series will hopefully be complete by 2027. At the very beginning we had not considered including variant texts or French versions, but an urge to completeness quickly took over the project, and all volumes have subsequently included French variants for original Spanish poems and vice versa, provided they were by the author, or could viably be ascribed to him. Last year we issued a new edition of *Equatorial and other poems* (the first edition also originally appeared in 2019) to include a French version of the long title poem, perhaps the author's most significant work prior to 1931; it seemed only right to apply the same principle to *Skyquake*, and bring it into line with the rest of the series. A number of changes have been made to the text of the original translation, in some cases to make things a little clearer, but also, in some cases, to correct errors.

---

[3] Óscar Hahn, *Vicente Huidobro o el atentado celeste*, Madrid: Visor Libros, 2018.

§ § §

On a more personal note, I first became interested in Huidobro—until then little more than a name to me—while living in Chile in the early 1990s. My sojourn in Santiago happened to coincide with the centenary of the poet's birth and the appearance of a number of publications, all of which served to offer an intriguing introduction to his work. It was only later that I explored *Temblor* in any great detail—the text was at that point only to be found in an out of print *Obras completas* [Complete Works]—having previously been obsessed, like so many others, by the other work published in 1931, *Altazor*. The latter remains perhaps the more fascinating work, partly because it is such a recognisable modernist monument. By contrast, *Temblor* has had relatively little attention, but it deserves to sit alongside the longer verse masterpiece as Huidobro's crowning achievement. Looking back from the vantage point of 2025, it seems odd that *Temblor* only appeared in Chile in 1942, eleven years after the first Madrid edition, but it was an unfortunate fact that the author's poetry was under-appreciated in his own country for many years. At the time of his death in 1948, very little was in print, and *Altazor* was not to be published in Santiago until 1949.

The works that followed *Temblor* were much calmer—they could scarcely have been more frenetic—taking a different poetic direction, but this was an author who could not be pinned down, one who kept moving, kept staying ahead of all waves and movements. He was his own man to the very end, and we are all the better for it.

Tony Frazer
2019; revised, 2025

TEMBLOR DE CIELO

SKYQUAKE

Ante todo hay que saber cuántas veces debemos abandonar nuestra novia y huir de sexo en sexo hasta el fin de la tierra.

Allí en donde el vacío pasa su arco de violín sobre el horizonte y el hombre se transforma en pájaro y el ángel en piedra preciosa.

El Padre Eterno está fabricando tinieblas en su laboratorio y trabaja para volver sordos a los ciegos. Tiene un ojo en la mano y no sabe a quién ponérselo. Y en un bocal tiene una oreja en cópula con otro ojo.

Estamos lejos, en el fin de los fines, en donde un hombre colgado por los pies de una estrella se balancea en el espacio con la cabeza hacia abajo. El viento que dobla los árboles, agita sus cabellos dulcemente.

Los arroyos voladores se posan en las selvas nuevas donde los pájaros maldicen el amanecer de tanta flor inútil.

Con cuánta razón ellos insultan las palpitaciones de esas cosas oscuras.

Si se tratara solamente de degollar al capitán de las flores y hacerle sangrar el corazón del sentimiento superfluo, el corazón lleno de secretos y trozos de universo.

La boca de un hombre amado sobre un tambor.

Los senos de la niña inolvidable clavados en el mismo árbol donde los picotean los ruiseñores.

Y la estatua del héroe en el polo.

Destruirlo todo, todo, a bala y a cuchillo.

Los ídolos se baten bajo el agua.

—Isolda, Isolda, cuántos kilómetros nos separan, cuántos sexos entre tú y yo.

Tú sabes bien que Dios arranca los ojos a las flores, pues su manía es la ceguera.

Y transforma el espíritu en un paquete de plumas y transforma las novias sentadas sobre rosas en serpientes de pianola, en serpientes hermanas de la flauta, de la misma flauta que se besa en las noches de nieve y que las llama desde lejos.

Pero tú no sabes por qué razón el mirlo despedaza el árbol entre sus dedos sangrientos.

Y éste es el misterio.

Cuarenta días y cuarenta noches trepando de rama en rama como en el Diluvio. Cuarenta días y cuarenta noches de misterio entre rocas y picachos.

Yo podría caerme de destino en destino, pero siempre guardaré el recuerdo del cielo.

First of all it should be known how often we must abandon our bride and flee from sex to sex right to the ends of the earth.

There where the void draws its violin bow over the horizon and a man turns into a bird and an angel into a precious stone.

The Eternal Father is fashioning darkness in his laboratory where he strives to turn blind men deaf. He keeps one eye in his hand and knows not on whom he should pin it. And in a jar he keeps an ear coupling with another eye.

We are far away, at the end of all things where a man, hanging by his feet from a star, swings head-down in space. The wind that bends the trees gently ruffles his hair.

Flying streams settle in new forests where birds curse the appearance of so many useless flowers.

How right they are to insult the fluttering of these dark things.

If it were only a matter of slitting the throat of the captain of flowers and making his heart bleed with superfluous feelings, a heart full of secrets and shards of the universe.

The mouth of a beloved man upon a drum.

The breasts of the unforgettable girl nailed to the same tree where they are pecked at by nightingales.

And the hero's statue at the Pole.

Destroy all of it, all of it, with bullet and blade.

Idols fight it out under water.

—Isolde, Isolde, how many kilometres separate us, how many sexes between you and me.

You well know that God plucks out the eyes of flowers, for he is obsessed with blindness.

And he turns the spirit into a bundle of feathers and turns brides seated on roses into pianola snakes, into snakes that are sister to the flute, the same flute that is kissed on snowy nights and that calls them from afar.

But you do not know why the blackbird shreds the tree with its bloody talons.

And this is the mystery.

Forty days and forty nights climbing from branch to branch as in the days of the Flood. Forty days and forty nights of mystery amongst rocks and peaks.

I could fall from destiny to destiny, but I will always retain the memory of the sky.

¿Conoces las visiones de la altura? ¿Has visto el corazón de la luz? Yo me convierto a veces en una selva inmensa y recorro los mundos como un ejército.

Mira la entrada de los ríos.

El mar puede apenas ser mi teatro en ciertas tardes.

La calle de los sueños no tiene árboles, ni una mujer crucificada en una flor, ni un barco pasando las páginas del mar.

La calle de los sueños tiene un ombligo inmenso de donde asoma una botella. Adentro de la botella hay un obispo muerto que cambia de colores cada vez que se mueve la botella.

Hay cuatro velas que se encienden y se apagan siguiendo un turno sucesivo. A veces un relámpago nos hace ver en el cielo una mujer despedazada que viene cayendo desde hace ciento cuarenta años.

El cielo esconde su misterio.

En todas las escalas se supone un asesino escondido. Los cantores cardíacos mueren sólo de pensar en ello.

Así las mariposas enfermizas volverán a su estado de gusanos, del cual no debían haber salido nunca. El oído recaerá en infancia y se llenará de ecos marinos y de esas algas que flotan en los ojos de ciertos pájaros.

Solamente Isolda conoce el misterio. Pero ella recorre el arco iris con sus dedos temblorosos en busca de un sonido especial.

Y si un mirlo le picotea el ojo, ella le deja beber toda el agua que quiera con la misma sonrisa que atrae los rebaños de búfalos.

¿Sobre qué corazón hinchado de amargura podrías flotar tú en todos los océanos, en cualquier mar?

Porque debes saber que aferrarse a un corazón como a una boya es peligroso a causa de las grutas marinas que los atraen y en donde los pulpos que son nudos de serpientes o trompas de elefantes les cierran la salida para siempre.

Date cuenta de lo que es una montaña con los brazos levantados pidiendo perdón y piensa que es menos peligrosa que los mares y más asequible a la amistad.

Sin embargo, tu destino es amar lo peligroso, lo peligroso que hay en ti y fuera de ti, besar los labios del abismo contando con ayudas tenebrosas para el triunfo final de todas tus empresas y tus sueños cubiertos de rocío en el amanecer.

De lo contrario agradece y retírate hasta el fondo de la memoria de los hombres.

Have you experienced visions from on high? Have you seen the heart of the light? Sometimes I turn into a vast forest and march across worlds like an army.

Look at the river mouth.

On some evenings the sea can hardly even serve as my theatre.

The street of dreams has no trees, no woman crucified in a flower, no boat sailing the pages of the sea.

The street of dreams has an enormous navel from which a bottle protrudes. Inside the bottle there is a dead bishop who changes colour whenever the bottle moves.

There are four candles that light up and go out one after the other. Sometimes a flash of lightning reveals in the sky a dismembered woman who has been falling for one hundred and forty years.

The sky conceals its mystery.

On every stairway one suspects a hidden killer. Faint-hearted singers die at the very thought of it.

So it is that sickly butterflies will return to the caterpillar state they should never have left. The ear will relapse into childhood and will be filled with marine echoes and that seaweed which floats in the eyes of some birds.

Only Isolde knows the mystery. But she runs her trembling fingers along the rainbow seeking a special sound.

And if a blackbird pecks at her eye, she lets it drink as much water as it wants, with the same smile that attracts herds of buffalo.

On which heart, swollen with bitterness, could you float on all the oceans, on any sea?

Surely you must know that clinging to a heart like a buoy is dangerous because of the sea caves that attract them, where octopi like knots of snakes or elephant trunks block the exit forever.

Realise what a mountain is like, with its arms raised, begging forgiveness, and bear in mind that it is less dangerous than the seas and more amenable to friendship.

However it is your destiny to love danger, the danger that lies within you and without you, to kiss the lips of the abyss, relying on shadowy forces for the final triumph of all your ventures and your dreams, drenched with dew at daybreak.

If not, give thanks and withdraw into the depths into of mankind's memory.

—Isolda, Isolda, en la época glacial los osos eran flores. Cuando vino el deshielo se libertaron de sí mismos y salieron corriendo en todas direcciones.

Piensa en la resurrección.

Sólo tú conoces el milagro. Tú has visto ejecutarse el milagro ante cien arpas maravilladas y todos los cañones apuntando al horizonte.

Había entonces un desfile de marineros ante un rey en un país lejano. Las olas esperaban impacientes la vuelta de los suyos. Entretanto el mar aplaudía.

El termómetro bajaba lentamente porque el mirlo había dejado de cantar y pensaba lanzarse de un trapecio al medio del mundo.

Ahora sólo una cosa temo y es que tú salgas de una lámpara o de algún florero y me hables en términos elocuentes como hablan las magnolias en la tarde. El cuarto se llenaría de libélulas agonizantes y yo tendría que sentarme para no caer al suelo sin conocimiento.

La muerte sería el pensamiento mismo. Reflejado en todas partes donde se vuelvan los ojos.

Sobre el castillo el esqueleto del general hará señas como un semáforo. Nosotros contaremos las calaveras que se arrastran por el campo atadas a través de una cuerda interminable a la cola del caballo sonámbulo que nadie reconoce como suyo.

Los esclavos negros aplaudirán sobre el vientre de las esclavas tan ebrias como ellos sin darse cuenta de que el viento es un fantasma y que los árboles allá lejos flotan sobre un cementerio.

¿Quién ha contado todos sus muertos?

¿Y si se abrieran todas las ventanas y si todas las lámparas se ponen a cantar y si se incendia el cementerio?

Por cada pájaro del cielo habrá un cazador en la tierra.

Sonarán los clarines y las banderas se convertirán en luces de Bengala. Murió la fe, murieron todas las aves de rapiña que te roían el corazón.

Pasan volando las estatuas migratorias.

En la llanura inmensa se oye el suplicio de los ídolos entre los cantos de los árboles.

Las flores huyen despavoridas.

Se abren las puertas de una música desconocida y salen los años del mago que se queda sentado agonizando con las manos sobre el pecho.

Cuántas cosas han muerto adentro de nosotros. Cuánta muerte llevamos en nosotros. ¿Porqué aferramos a nuestros muertos? ¿Porqué nos empeñ-

—Isolde, Isolde, in the Ice Age bears were flowers. When the thaw came they freed themselves and ran off in all directions.

Think of the resurrection.

You alone know the miracle. You have seen the miracle performed in the presence of a hundred astonished harps and all the cannons aimed at the horizon.

There was then a procession of sailors before a king in a far-off land. The waves impatiently awaited their return, while the sea applauded.

The thermometer dropped slowly because the blackbird had stopped singing and was thinking of leaping from a trapeze at the centre of the world.

Now I fear only one thing and it is that you might emerge from a lamp or some vase and speak to me in eloquent terms the way magnolias speak in the evening. The room would be filled with dying dragonflies and I would have to sit down so as not to faint.

Death would be thought itself. Reflected everywhere the eyes might turn.

Above the castle the general's skeleton will signal like a semaphore. We will count the skulls being dragged across the field, tied by an endless rope to the tail of a sleepwalking horse that no-one claims as their own.

Black slaves will applaud over the bellies of slave women, so intoxicated that they do not realize the wind is a ghost and the trees are floating above a cemetery, far away.

Who has counted all their dead?

And if all the windows were opened and all the lamps began to sing and the cemetery caught fire?

For every bird in the sky there will be a hunter on the ground.

Bugles will sound and flags will turn into sparklers. Faith is dead; dead too are the birds of prey that gnawed at your heart.

Migrating statues fly by.

On the vast plain the torment of idols can be heard amidst the singing trees.

Flowers flee in terror.

The doors of an unknown music open and out come the years of the sorcerer who remains seated in his agony, hands on his chest.

How many things have died inside us. How much death we carry inside us. Why do we cling to our dead? Why do we persist in reviving

amos en resucitar nuestros muertos? Ellos nos impiden ver la idea que nace. Tenemos miedo a la nueva luz que se presenta, a la que no estamos habituados todavía como a nuestros muertos inmóviles y sin sorpresa peligrosa. Hay que dejar lo muerto por lo que vive.

—Isolda, entierra todos tus muertos.

Piensa, recuerda, olvida. Que tu recuerdo olvide sus recuerdos, que tu olvido recuerde sus olvidos. Cuida de no morir antes de tu muerte.

Cómo dar un poco de grandeza a esta bestia actual que sólo dobla sus rodillas de cansancio a esas altas horas en que la luna llega volando y se coloca al frente.

Y, sin embargo, vivimos esperando un azar, la formación de un signo sideral en ese expiatorio más allá, en donde no alcanza a llegar ni el sonido de nuestras campanas.

Así, esperando el gran azar.

Que el polo norte se desprenda como el sombrero que saluda.

Que surja el continente que estamos aguardando desde hace tantos años, aquí sentados detrás de las rejas del horizonte.

Que pase corriendo el asesino disparando balazos sin control a sus perseguidores.

Que se sepa por qué nació aquella niña y no el niño prometido por los sueños y anunciado tantas veces.

Que se vea el cadáver que bosteza y se estira debajo de la tierra.

Que se vea pasar el fantasma glorioso entre las arboledas del cielo.

Que de repente se detengan todos los ríos a una voz de mando.

Que el cielo cambie de lugar.

Que los mares se amontonen en una gran pirámide más alta que todas las babeles soñadas por la ambición.

Que sople un viento desesperado y apague las estrellas.

Que un dedo luminoso escriba una palabra en el cielo de la noche.

Que se derrumbe la casa de enfrente.

Para esto vivimos, puedes creerme, para esto vivimos y no para otra cosa. Para esto tenemos voz y para esto tenemos una red en la voz.

Y para esto tenemos ese correr angustiado adentro de las venas y ese galope de animal herido en el pecho.

Para esto enrojece la carne martirizada de las palabras y crece el pensamiento regado por los ríos subterráneos. Para esto el aullido del sobresalto heredado del abuelo más trágico.

our dead? They prevent us from seeing ideas being born. We fear the new light that comes along – one we are not yet accustomed to, as we are to our motionless dead, who lack dangerous surprises. The dead have to be left behind for the sake of the living.

—Isolde, bury all your dead.

Think, remember, forget. May your memory forget your memories, may your forgetfulness remember what is forgotten. Take care not to die before your death.

How does one grant a little greatness to this present-day creature that only bends its weary knees at this late hour when the moon comes flying in and stands before you.

And yet we live in hope of some chance occurrence, the appearance of an astral sign in that expiatory beyond, where not even the sound of our bells manages to penetrate.

Waiting, in this way, for the great chance.

Let the North Pole come off like a hat raised in greeting.

Let the continent emerge, the one we have awaited so many years, while sitting here behind the bars of the horizon.

Let the killer run past, firing wild shots at his pursuers.

Let it be known why that girl was born and not the boy promised in dreams and foretold so many times.

Let the corpse appear yawning and stretching beneath the earth.

Let the glorious ghost be seen passing through the groves of heaven.

Let all rivers be halted suddenly by a single command.

Let the sky change location.

Let the seas pile up into a great pyramid higher than all the Babels dreamed of by ambition.

Let a desperate wind blow and extinguish the stars.

Let a luminous finger write a word in the night sky.

Let the house across the street collapse.

For this do we live, believe me, for this do we live and for nothing else. For this we have a voice and for this our voice has a net.

And for this we have that anguished racing in our veins and that wounded animal galloping in our chest.

For this the flesh of words reddens in martyrdom, and thought grows, watered by underground rivers. That is why we have inherited the howl of shock from the most tragic of our ancestors.

Cortad la cabeza al monstruo que ruge en la puerta del sueño. Y luego que nadie prohiba nada.

Alguien habla y nace una amapola en la cumbre de la voz antes que brille el opio de la mirada futura.

—Paz en la tierra al marinero de la noche.

Los exploradores silenciosos levantan la cabeza y la aventura se desnuda de su traje de oro.

He aquí el sentido del ocaso.

Acaso el ocaso nos haga caso y entonces habréis comprendido los signos de la noche. Habréis comprendido los inventos del silencio. La mirada del sueño. El umbral del abismo. El viaje de los montes.

La travesía de la noche.

Isolda, Isolda, yo sigo mi destino.

¿En dónde has escondido el oasis que me habías prometido tantas veces?

La luz se cansó de andar.

¿A dónde lleva, dime, esa escalera que sale de tus ojos y se pierde en el aire?

¿Sabes tú que mi destino es andar? ¿Conoces la vanidad del explorador y el fantasma de la aventura?

Es una cuestión de sangre y huesos frente a un imán especial. Es un destino irrevocable de meteoro fabuloso.

No es una cuestión de amor en carne, es una cuestión de vida, una cuestión de espíritu viajante, de pájaro nómade.

Todas esas mujeres son árboles o piedras de reposo en el camino tal vez innecesarias.

Botellas de agua o toneles de embriaguez generalmente sin luz propia. Obedecen como las catedrales a un principio musical. Cada acorde tiene su correspondiente y todo consiste en saber tocar el punto del eco que ha de responder. Es fácil hacer tejidos de sones y construir una verdadera techumbre o magníficas cúpulas para los días de lluvia.

Si el destino lo permite, podemos guarecernos por un tiempo y contar los dedos de aquella que nos tiende los brazos.

Luego el fantasma nos obligará a seguir la marcha. Saltaremos por encima de los senos palpitantes que son sus cúpulas, porque ella tendida de espaldas imita un templo. Mejor dicho son los templos los que la imitan a ella, con sus torres como senos, su cúpula central como cabeza y su puerta

Cut off the head of the monster roaring at dream's door. And then let no-one forbid anything.

Someone speaks and a poppy appears at the voice's pinnacle before the opium of the future gaze can shine.

—Peace on earth to the night sailor.

Silent explorers raise their heads and the adventure is stripped of its golden costume.

This is the meaning of sunset.

Perhaps the sunset will heed us and then you will have understood the signs of the night. You will have understood the inventions of silence. The gaze of dreams. The threshold of the abyss. The journey through the mountains.

The crossing of the night.

Isolde, Isolde, I am following my destiny.

Where did you hide the oasis you promised me so many times?

The light grew weary of moving.

Tell me, where does that stairway lead, the one that leaves your eyes and then vanishes into the air?

Do you know it is my destiny to walk? Do you recognise the explorer's vanity and the ghost of adventure?

It is a matter of flesh and blood being confronted by a special magnet. It is an irrevocable destiny for a meteor out of legend.

It is not a matter of fleshly love, it is a matter of life, a matter of a travelling spirit, of a nomadic bird.

All those women are trees, or resting stones along the path, perhaps none of them necessary.

Bottles of water or barrels of inebriation, mostly without their own light. Like cathedrals, they adhere to a musical principle. Each chord has its counterpart and everything depends on knowing how to strike the echo point, which has to respond. It is simple to weave sounds together and construct a genuine roof or magnificent domes for rainy days.

If destiny so permits, we can take refuge for a while and count the fingers of whoever holds her arms out to us.

After that the ghost will force us to proceed. We will leap over the beating breasts that form their domes because, lying on her back, she is like a temple. Or rather, it is a case of temples imitating her, with their breast-like towers, their central dome like a head, and their doorway that seeks

que quisiera imitar al sexo por donde se entra a buscar la vida que late en el vientre y por donde debe salir después la misma vida.

Pero nosotros no hemos de aceptar semejante imitación, ni podemos creer en la tal vida. En esa vida que sale con los ojos vendados y va estrellándose en todos los árboles del paisaje. Sólo creeremos en las flores que son cunas de gigantes, aunque sabemos que adentro de cada capullo duerme un enano.

Y al fondo las montañas de roca viva sonríen dulcemente.

Las montañas sonríen porque un ciego se ha sentado encima de ellas a oír redoblar los tambores del volcán. Pero lo que pasa en los llanos es más importante aún, pues los árboles del bosque se han convertido en serpientes y se debaten rítmicamente a causa de una flauta especial.

Me olvidaba deciros que también hay un lago y que este lago se aleja según la dirección del viento. A veces llega hasta a perderse de vista, a veces pasa largos años ausente y vuelve de otro color. A veces tiene hambre y maldice a los hombres que no naufragan a la hora debida. Otras veces camina en cuatro patas y roe durante horas y horas los despojos de tanta tragedia acumulados en sus orillas o los reflejos de quién sabe qué tiempos secretos.

Si el pájaro del ojo se cae en el lago, salta un geyser en la montaña. Un geyser hermoso como un árbol con una mujer que se equilibra en la punta.

También el lago puede equilibrarse en la punta del árbol. Todo depende de mi voluntad y del tambor que redoble a tiempo.

Todos esos espías escondidos tras los árboles no esperan el milagro como ellos quisieran hacer creer, sino a la mujer desnuda y ciega que sale a pasear en las tardes su estatua perdida y puede estrellarse en ellos.

Estás malgastando el tiempo.

Mirad, mirad, hay un incendio en la luna.

Vestida de blanco, Isolda venía como una nube. Entonces la luna empezó a caer envuelta en llamas. En las playas danzaba un reflejo de fuego.

Los espectros salen uno a uno de cada ola que se levanta. Vosotros que estáis allí escondidos, llegó la hora de temblar ante la voracidad de la muerte.

El sol poniente hace una aureola sobre la cabeza del último náufrago que flota a la deriva sin oír más los cantos de la orilla.

Los lobos se pasean con los ojos brillantes entre las ramas de la noche, en lazados estrechamente y llorando sin causa precisa.

El hombre aquel, más grande que los otros, abre la boca en medio del jardín y empieza a tragar luciérnagas durante horas enteras.

to imitate the vulva where one enters looking for the life that pulses in the womb and through which life itself later issues forth.

But we do not have to accept such imitations, nor can we believe in such a life. In this life which emerges, blindfolded, and crashes into all the trees in the countryside. We will only believe in flowers that are cradles for giants, although we know that inside each bud there sleeps a dwarf.

And in the background the mountains of living rock smile sweetly.

The mountains smile because a blind man has sat down on their peaks to hear the drumming of the volcano. But what happens on the plains is more important, for the trees in the forest have turned into snakes, writhing rhythmically to the sound of a special flute.

I forgot to tell you there is also a lake, and that this lake moves away, pushed by the wind. Sometimes it is even lost from view, sometimes it is gone for long years and returns a different colour. Sometimes it is hungry and curses men who fail to be shipwrecked at the appointed hour. Other times it walks on all fours and gnaws for hours and hours on the scraps of so much tragedy washed up on its shores or on the reflections of who knows what secret times.

If the bird in the eye falls into the lake, a geyser erupts in the mountains. A geyser beautiful as a tree, with a woman balancing at its tip.

The lake too can balance on top of the tree. Everything depends on my will and on the drum beating in time.

All those spies hiding behind trees are not waiting for the miracle, as they would have us believe, but for the naked blind woman who emerges in the evening to take her lost statue for a walk and who might collide with them.

You are wasting time.

Look, look, there is a fire on the moon.

Dressed in white, Isolde arrived like a cloud. Then the moon began to fall, enveloped in flames. On the beaches there danced a reflection of fire.

Spectres emerged one by one from every rising wave. You who are hidden there, the hour has come to tremble before the voracity of death.

The setting sun forms a halo over the head of the last shipwrecked sailor, who floats adrift unable to hear any singing from the shore.

Wolves roam with glowing eyes amidst the foliage of night, bound tightly together and weeping for no real reason.

That man there, taller than the others, opens his mouth in the middle of the garden and begins swallowing fireflies for hour after hour.

Los árboles están retorcidos a causa de un dolor extraño. Y millares de meteoros que caen del cielo forman espirales en la atmósfera nuestra como si fueran piedras en el agua.

Un humo espeso sale de todos lados. Ahora sólo brillan los ojos de los lobos y el hombre lleno de luciérnagas. Todo lo demás es penumbra.

La montaña abre sus puertas y el ciego entra con los brazos extendidos.

Hay un árbol, un árbol grueso que se retuerce en el fuego del crepúsculo.

Arriba se está meciendo un planeta recién nacido.

Caen aureolas sobre la tierra. Una detrás de otra van cayendo cientos de aureolas sobre la tierra, algunas sobre ciertas cabezas … ¿Y nada más?

Una isla de palmeras surge del mar para los novios que se pasean enlazados.

Algún día uno de ellos encontrará la cabeza que se le había perdido, inmóvil en el mismo sitio en que la perdiera.

¿Cuándo? ¿En dónde? ¿Cuál de ellos?

He ahí el suplicio, Isolda, detrás de la montaña. He allí el suplicio.

Las selvas migratorias no llegarán tan lejos. Hay una sandalia sola en medio de la tierra.

La marcha de las tardes que pasan se siente en el fondo del mar. En el momento éste en que todo se torna brillante de ebriedad.

Hay un sombrero más allá a la altura de una cabeza.

Hay un bastón clavado en el suelo y a la altura de una mano.

Y no hay nada más. Porque ninguno de vosotros puede ver el fantasma que sonríe al perro en este instante.

Ninguno sabe por qué se movieron las cortinas detrás de la cama.

Ni por qué se sonrojaron las mejillas de Isolda como dos cortinas que se corren.

Y por qué temblaron sus piernas como dos cortinas que se abren.

* * *

Yo sería capaz de llorar en el amanecer por verte sonreír.

Sería capaz de mendigar el saludo del espectro que camina solemne hacia la edad de la piedra.

Bien lo sabes, por ti pasaré como un reflejo de selva en selva. ¿Qué más quieres?

Dos cuerpos enlazados domestican la eternidad.

The trees are twisted by a strange pain. And thousands of meteors falling from the sky create spirals in our atmosphere as if they were stones thrown into the water.

Thick smoke billows everywhere. Now the only things that glow are the eyes of wolves and the man full of fireflies. All the rest is gloom.

The mountain opens its doors and the blind man enters with outstretched arms.

There is a tree, a massive tree writhing in the fire of dusk.

Up above a newborn planet is being rocked.

Halos fall upon the earth. One after another hundreds of halos fall upon the earth, some of them onto heads … And nothing else?

An island of palm trees surges up from the sea for the newly-weds walking arm in arm.

One day one of them will find the head that they had lost, motionless in the very place where it had been lost.

When? Where? Which one of them?

There lies torment, Isolde, beyond the mountain. There lies torment.

The migrating forests will not get that far.

There is a solitary sandal at the centre of the earth.

The passage of evenings can be sensed at the bottom of the sea. At this moment when everything glows with intoxication.

There is a hat over there at head height.

There is a staff driven into the soil, at hand height.

And there is nothing more. Because none of you can see the ghost smiling at the dog at this moment.

No one knows why the curtains behind the bed moved.

Nor why Isolde's cheeks blushed like two curtains being drawn.

And why her legs trembled like two curtains being opened.

* * *

Upon waking, I could weep to see you smile.

I could beg a greeting from the spectre that is headed solemnly for the Stone Age.

This you know well, for you I will pass like a reflection from forest to forest. What more do you want?

Two bodies entwined tame eternity.

Y es preciso ponerse de rodillas.

Entonces el castillo se convierte en una flor, el ojo se convierte en un río lleno de barcas y toda clase de peces.

El piano se convierte en una montaña, el mar en una pequeña alcachofa que gira como un molino.

Los nervios se convierten en un árbol lleno de temblores y sus temblores se propagan en la noche de trecho en trecho hasta el infinito.

El cerebro rueda cuerpo abajo y se va no se sabe dónde. Al mismo instante las selvas huyen a la desbandada.

Empieza el suplicio de los huesos con su saco de nubes a cuestas, bajando desde la cumbre de la matriz silenciosa, triste como el pájaro de una bruja, como la flor amenazada en la noche.

Preparado por la soledad todo es posible. Desde luego, colgada de cada lámpara una mujer se mece en el aire que respiramos. Sale una música de cada cuadro en la pared, puesto que sabemos que todo paisaje es un instrumento musical. Y detrás de cada puerta hay un esqueleto impaciente que espera.

La noche llora en su retiro completamente abandonada. La noche que te auscultaba el corazón. La noche, ¿te acuerdas? Cuando las cortinas tomaban forma de orejas y forma de párpados con pestañas de silencio. Entonces yo me inclinaba sobre ti como en una mesa de disección, hundía en ti mis labios y te miraba; tu vientre semejante a una herida viva y tus ojos como el fin del mundo.

Arrastrados por la soledad, Isolda, nos sumergimos en la noche que nos esperaba al pie de la casa.

* * *

Hemos andado mucho. Los reflectores buscaban desesperados en la noche, corrían de un lado para otro, se cruzaban en el infinito, se saludaban y se despedían para siempre. De pronto una mano salió en medio del cielo, una mano como de náufrago, y apretó entre sus dedos la cabeza de un pájaro que cayó, sin una protesta de sus labios, lentamente sobre la tierra.

Estábamos a la orilla del mar. Una ola vino corriendo, tomó el pájaro muerto y se lo llevó consigo.

And they have to get down on their knees.

Then the castle turns into a flower, the ear into a river full of boats and all kinds of fish.

The piano turns into a mountain, the sea into a little artichoke that spins like a windmill.

The nerves turn into a tree full of tremors and its tremors multiply repeatedly through the night until infinity.

The brain rolls down the body and vanishes who knows where. At the same moment the forests flee in disorder.

The ordeal of the bones begins with sacks of clouds on their backs, coming down from the peak of the silent womb, sad as a witch's bird, sad as the flower threatened during the night.

Prepared by solitude, everything is possible. Of course, hanging from each chandelier, a woman swings through the air we breathe. Music emerges from every picture on the wall, since we know that every landscape is a musical instrument. And behind each door there is an impatient skeleton waiting.

Completely abandoned in its retreat, the night weeps. The night that sounded your heart. The night—do you remember?—when curtains took on the shape of ears and the shape of eyelids with silent lashes. Then I leaned over you as if over a dissecting table, sank my lips into you and watched you; your belly resembling a fresh wound and your eyes like the end of the world.

Dragged down by solitude, Isolde, we sank into the night that awaited us at the foot of the house.

* * *

We walked a great deal. Searchlights scanned desperately through the night, from one side to the other, and crossed paths at infinity, greeted one another and then said their farewells forever. Suddenly a hand appeared in the midst of the sky, a hand like that of a castaway, and crushed between its fingers the head of a bird that fell slowly to the ground, with no protest from its lips.

We were by the sea. A wave came rushing in, took the dead bird and carried it away.

La montaña de la orilla tuvo un pequeño escalofrío, luego de su espalda de cetáceo brotó un chorro de agua fresca y cristalina mientras una ola pasaba por encima del faro que pareció adentro de una vitrina lejana.

Así volvió la hora de la serenidad traída de la mano por un cometa que nadie supo bautizar y que los niños llamaron, nunca se ha sabido por qué, Cabellera de Eloísa.

Aún suele verse en las noches el ojo que flota sobre el mar como una almendra desolada.

Aún suele verse el barco que pasa por el aire con las redes tendidas.

Aún suele verse al ahogado mecido entre dos aguas con el cuerpo luminoso.

Aún suele verse el velero como una cruz en su Gólgota interminable.

Aún suele verse a los piratas aferrados a la quilla y al capitán colgado del palo mayor en alta mar.

Aún puede verse a la luz de un relámpago al timonero pálido con las barbas al viento.

Aún puede verse a la luz de un relámpago a la muerta desnuda con los senos hinchados.

Aún puede verse a la luz de un relámpago el caballo del rapto que se pierde a lo lejos.

Aún suele verse en las noches de luna la mano que flota.

Pero la pesca de sirenas con los cabellos enredados en las redes no ha vuelto a verse y en vano hemos esperado.

Hemos saludado todas las olas, hemos mirado atentamente, hemos agitado nuestros sombreros y nuestros pañuelos, hemos jugado sus senos a los dados en la cubierta de miles de barcos. Todo inútil. Los cómplices del alba oyeron las flores en viaje, oyeron la marcha de la luz polar y otra vez la marcha del héroe hacia la edad de piedra.

Pero nadie verá el suplicio de las sirenas.

En vano levantáis los dedos señalando cada pliegue del mar o cada temblor en las nubes.

Yo os lo digo, ella está más escondida que la noche.

Un pájaro solitario como el mar se aleja lentamente, tal vez a causa de vuestros gritos.

Se aleja lentamente, he dicho, hacia las maravillas de su sueño propio. Se aleja llevándose el sentido de la tarde.

The mountain by the shore shivered slightly, and then from its cetacean back spouted a jet of fresh, crystalline water while a wave rolled over the lighthouse, which appeared to be inside a distant display case.

Thus returned the hour of serenity, led by the hand of a comet that no-one knew what to name and that the children called, no-one ever knew why, Eloise's Hair.

Sometimes, at night, the eye can still be seen floating on the sea like a desolate almond.

Sometimes the trawler can still be seen passing through the air with its nets extended.

Sometimes the drowned man can still be seen rocked between two waters, his body glowing.

Sometimes the sailing boat can still be seen like a cross on its never-ending Golgotha.

Sometimes pirates can still be seen clinging to the keel and their captain hanging from the mainmast on the open sea.

In a flash of lightning, the pale helmsman can still be seen, his beard in the wind.

In a flash of lightning, the naked beauty can still be seen, her breasts swollen.

In a flash of lightning, the kidnapper's horse can still be seen vanishing into the distance.

Sometimes, on moonlit nights, the floating hand can still be seen.

But mermaids, fishing with their hair meshed into nets have not been seen again, and we have waited in vain.

We have greeted all the waves, watched attentively, waved our hats and our handkerchiefs, gambled their breasts at dice on board thousands of ships. All in vain. Dawn's accomplices heard the flowers on their journey, heard the progress of the polar light and once again the hero's advance towards the Stone Age.

But no-one will see the ordeal of the mermaids.

In vain do you raise your fingers, pointing to every fold in the sea and every tremor in the clouds.

I tell you, she is better hidden than the night.

A bird, solitary as the sea, flies off slowly, perhaps because of your cries.

It flies off slowly, I said, to the wonders of its own slumber. It flies off carrying with it the sense of evening.

No es para vosotros el panorama del secreto naciente. ¿Qué sabéis vosotros de los encuentros en la eternidad?

Os repito, ella está más escondida que la noche al mediodía.

Inútilmente aparejamos hacia la venturosa exploración. Ni hacia las pescas impasibles apenas iluminadas por las luces internas del mar, apenas balanceadas por el silencio o la soledad.

* * *

¿Quién ha sido el asesino?

Ante el juez está el cadáver de la mujer como la momia de la más bella faraona.

Gritad, acusadores.

Inútilmente el juez escruta los ojos de los circunstantes. La forma de ningún ojo presente corresponde a la forma de la herida que se ve aún sangrienta en el pecho desnudo.

Una ráfaga violenta cierra todos los párpados. El juez enrojece de cólera.

—Señores ¿quién oyó el disparo? ¿Nadie vio una sombra huir por la ventana? ¿Nadie vio una luz en medio de la noche?

Todos los ojos se vuelven hacia el hombre grande que se comía las luciérnagas en el jardín.

A través de la transparencia de su cuerpo, se ve algo como un puñal o un lirio escondidos, pero la tranquilidad del presunto criminal siembra la duda en sus acusadores.

Dos lágrimas ruedan por sus mejillas.

—Es él, es él —gritan algunos.

—No es él, no es él —gritan otros.

Un redoble de tambores, viene bajando por el cielo como si cayera una lluvia de piedras en la luna.

El acusado permanece imperturbable. Con los ojos grandes fijos, sin un pestañeo, aun en el momento en que siente una corona que empieza a nacer en torno a su frente.

Todos miran hacia las calles. Va cruzando el cortejo brotado de la explosión triunfal. Las banderas desplegadas como el viento. Todos miran, pero él ni siquiera mueve los ojos.

—Al criminal. Al criminal.

Not for you the panorama of the emerging secret. What do you know of encounters in eternity?

I tell you again, she is better hidden than the night at mid-day.

Uselessly, we set the rigging for successful exploration. Not for the impassive catch barely lit by the sea's inner light, barely swayed by silence or solitude.

* * *

Who was the killer?

Before the judge lies the body of a woman like the mummy of the most beautiful of Pharaoh's wives.

Cry out, accusers.

In vain, the judge examines the eyes of those present. No eye present matches the shape of the wound that can still be seen bleeding on the bare chest.

A violent gust of wind closes all eyelids. The judge flushes with anger.

—Gentlemen, who heard the shot? Did no-one see a shadow escaping through the window? Did no-one see a light in the middle of the night?

All eyes return to the big man consuming fireflies in the garden.

Through his transparent body something like a hidden dagger or a lily can be seen, but the composure of the alleged criminal sows doubt in his accusers.

Two tears roll down his cheeks.

—He's the one, he's the one, some shout.

—It's not him, it's not him, shout others.

A drum-roll comes down from the sky as though a rain of stones were falling upon the moon.

The accused remains unmoved. With large unblinking eyes, steady even as he feels a crown beginning to form around his brow.

Everyone looks toward the street. The procession that erupted from the triumphant explosion crosses over. Banners unfurled like the wind. Everyone watches, but he doesn't even twitch an eye.

—Get the criminal. Get the criminal.

Cuando la muchedumbre se lanzó encima, mil puños levantados fueron a estrellarse en una estatua de mármol que miraba fijamente al horizonte.

Entonces en el horizonte apareció un cometa con un largo manto de luciérnagas y empezó a levantarse sobre el cielo, que lo recibía con los brazos abiertos.

A los pocos minutos, en el fondo del mismo horizonte se abrió una ventana y se asomó la novia con los ojos hermosos adormilados mirando al cometa y tratando de adivinar el presagio, acaso doloroso, que anunciaba su presencia entre los hombres. ¿Qué signos mágicos hace la novia con sus manos blancas como el cielo? Tiene en su mano derecha un diamante perfecto del cual empieza a brotar una fuente de aguas que corre mansa hacia nosotros.

De pronto un alarido ensordecedor se eleva en los aires.

—A la guillotina. La guillotina, la guillotina.

Momentos más tarde, cuando ante la muchedumbre sedienta de sangre el cuchillo fatal cortaba la cabeza de mármol del acusado, un inmenso chorro de luz manaba de su cuello interminablemente.

Al mismo instante hubo en el cielo un espantoso terremoto. Se rompían las estrellas en mil pedazos, se incendiaban los planetas, volaban trozos de lunas, saltaban carbones encendidos de los volcanes de otros astros y venían a veces a clavarse chirriando en los ojos desorbitados de los hombres.

La muchedumbre huía despavorida. Unos se escondían pidiendo auxilio bajo la tierra, otros caían de rodillas golpeándose el pecho y clamando perdón con los brazos levantados al firmamento.

El chorro de luz seguía manando del cuello del ajusticiado sobre la plataforma de la muerte.

* * *

En medio de la catástrofe y de la confusión general, unos brazos más poderosos que cien mares se apretaron en mi cuello.

—Isolda, Isolda, ¿eres tú?

—Cuántos años lejos el uno del otro.

—Se ha necesitado una hecatombe semejante para volver a encontrarnos.

—Tú, árbol de la sabiduría, con los ojos maduros en la puerta del sueño y ese andar de elefante con pies de ídolo.

When the mob lunged for him, a thousand raised fists smashed against a marble statue gazing fixedly at the horizon.

Then on the horizon a comet appeared with a long mantle of fireflies, and began to rise through the sky, which received it with open arms.

A few moments later, a window opened deep within the same horizon, and the bride with beautiful drowsy eyes came out to watch the comet, trying to decipher the omen, perhaps sorrowful, that its presence amongst mankind announced. What magical signs does the bride make with her sky-white hands? On her right hand she wears a perfect diamond from which a fountain of water begins to flow, running gently towards us.

Suddenly a deafening clamour rises into the air.

—To the guillotine. The guillotine, the guillotine.

Moments later, when the fateful blade had severed the marble head of the accused before the bloodthirsty mob, an enormous jet of light spurted unceasingly from his neck.

At that same moment there was a terrifying quake in the sky. Stars shattered into a thousand pieces, planets burst into flames, fragments of moons flew past, burning coals leaped from volcanoes on other worlds and sometimes landed sizzling in the bulging eyes of men.

The mob fled in terror. Some hid below ground, crying for help, others fell to their knees beating their breasts and begging forgiveness, arms raised to the heavens.

The jet of light kept welling up from the neck of the executed man on the gibbet.

* * *

Amidst the catastrophe and general confusion, arms more powerful than a hundred seas clutched at my neck.

—Isolde, Isolde, is that you?

—How many years we have been apart.

—It took carnage like this for us to meet again.

—You, tree of wisdom, with mature eyes at dream's door and that elephant-like gait with the feet of an idol.

A ver tus senos. Muéstrame los senos milenarios, tus senos del comienzo y del fin.

—Siempre esperando la edad de las maravillas como la paloma del mago.

—Dame a besar tus senos.

El ángel prisionero rompe sus cadenas y vuela en los aires perseguido, en vano, por algunos fusiles inexpertos.

Poderosa y solitaria vuelve a caer la noche. Las serpientes iluminadas de la tempestad corren a saltos en pos del ángel libertado imposible de atrapar.

Isolda se aprieta a mí, se incrusta entre mis brazos.

En la fragua de los relámpagos se oyen los martillazos con que la borrasca está labrando la corona para mi cabeza de rey.

¡Cuántos ciegos habrá hecho esta corona demasiado brillante!

Innumerables son los que al mirarla contemplan la última visión de su vida. El precioso gigante que agoniza sobre el mar, sólo pide mirarla para volver a la vida o morir tranquilo.

Son muchas las visiones grabadas en el la como en un friso. En el la se ve el cuerpo de una mujer ardiendo en el incendio que se levanta de sus propias carnes y no hay manera de apagar las llamas.

Y tantas otras visiones. Como aquel la de los enanos que pasan volando llevando sobre los hombros el ataúd de un Titán.

Y aquella de la isla arrancada por el viento que cae sobre la ciudad.

Y aquella del rayo entretejido en la lluvia de la borrasca.

Y aquella de las palmeras dobladas bajo las ruedas del huracán.

Y aquella de la montaña de nubes que se detiene tanto tiempo que empieza a crecer en ella una dulce vegetación.

Y aquella de la noche amarga en que se está muriendo alguien.

Creo que es llegado el momento de pensar en la noche en que nos estaremos muriendo nosotros.

Isolda, te amo y a través de todas las otras sólo he buscado amarte más.

Amarga es la noche y profundo el abismo donde tus brazos me arrojaron. Voy cayendo crispado con las manos desesperadas como un Niágara irremisiblemente perdido.

Las espumas me salpican el rostro antes de llegar al fondo. El ruido me aturde las orejas, me rebota en el cerebro antes de que mi cuerpo se rompa en pedazos en el fondo.

Sin embargo, aún sonrío esperando que de un momento a otro mi cuerpo puede sentirse más ligero que el aire.

Let me see your breasts. Show me those age-old breasts, your breasts of alpha and omega.

—Always waiting for the age of wonders like the magician's dove.

—Let me kiss your breasts.

The imprisoned angel breaks his chains and flies into the air, pursued in vain by a few unskilled shotguns.

Powerful, solitary, night began to fall again. The snakes illuminated by the storm bound forward, chasing the liberated angel, who is impossible to catch.

Isolde clings to me, embedded in my arms.

In the lightning-forge, hammering can be heard as the storm shapes the crown for my kingly head.

How many will be blinded by this all too brilliant crown!

Countless are those who, upon seeing it, behold the final vision of their lives. The handsome giant dying above the sea asks only to look upon it once more, so he might return to life or die in peace.

Many are the visions engraved upon it, as if on a frieze. The body of a woman can be seen there, burning in the fire rising from her own flesh, and there is no way of extinguishing the flames.

And so many other visions. Like that of dwarfs flying past, carrying on their shoulders the coffin of a Titan.

And that of the island snatched away by the wind falling onto the city.

And that of lightning interwoven with storm rains.

And that of palm trees bent beneath the wheels of the hurricane.

And that of the mountain of clouds that lingers so long that sweet greenery begins to grow upon it.

And that of the bitter night when someone is dying.

I believe that the moment has come to think of the night when we ourselves will die.

Isolde, I love you, and through all the others I have only sought to love you more.

Bitter is the night and deep the abyss where your arms hurled me. Convulsed, I fall, hands despairing, like a Niagara irretrievably lost.

The foam splashes my face before I reach the bottom. Noise deafens my ears, reverberates through my brain, before my body is dashed to pieces at the bottom.

I keep smiling nonetheless, hopeful that at any moment my body might feel lighter than air.

O que caiga un lazo de quién sabe qué estrella y me pesque y me levante en el momento mismo de ir a tocar el suelo.

—Isolda, he aquí la actitud del hombre perfecto.

El viento me mece de un lado para otro. Abajo, las miradas de los hombres me atan a su pavor terrestre en una llanura triste en la cual se ve una casa sola allá lejos y una humareda que trata de levantar la casa al cielo.

La casa del crimen jamás podrá despegarse de su pedazo de región. Sin embargo, a pesar de que el espectáculo ahora se ha puesto bastante lamentable, la noche es más brillante que nunca, no hay un puesto libre en todo el cielo. ¿Y esto para ver qué?

La garganta de la hermosa mujer tiene la forma de una canción.

Y ella cantará, cantará segura de que yo no he de morir aún. Cantará a pesar de la estación demasiado avanzada, a pesar de la noche que rueda de las montañas, a pesar de las dificultades del terreno. Cantará.

Y el niño dejará de llorar sobre su pequeño navío blanco. Y saldrá una estrella finísima encima de su cabeza, al fondo de la alcoba, más allá de sus almohadas sensibles, en los arrecifes verdaderos de su último sueño.

Tal vez oigamos la voz confundida en un canto enorme porque el mar está tendido sobre varias pianolas y a veces se abandona a sus propios instintos.

Entonces llega la hora de la transfiguración. El mar suda y se retuerce de un íntimo dolor. Cada ola se convierte en ángel y vuela.

¡Ay de aquel que osó levantar la mano sobre el mar!

Vosotros no lo sabéis y por eso os lo digo: en las noches, cuando nadie lo mira, el mar se convierte en un gran monumento y dicen que en la punta se alza de pie, solemne, la estatua de sí mismo.

Nadie sabrá nunca cuál es la verdad, ni tampoco el número de errores que maneja cada hombre en todos los instantes de su vida.

¿Sobre qué cantidad de errores descansa cada invento del hombre?

Esos inventos más hermosos que una chispa eléctrica y que las piernas de una mujer. Aquí se inclinan todos los sabios, aquí se arrodillan los profetas, aquí canta el gallo y donde termina su canto nace un paisaje como todos sabéis. Después sólo se ven las manos de los náufragos aferradas a las olas y una botella que flota y se aleja para contar la historia de tanta angustia.

¡Isolda, si tú supieras!

El cielo ha cambiado siete veces. Y volverá a cambiar a causa del mar. Porque el mar se ha convertido en globo y soltó sus amarras y se fue por el cielo.

Or that a lasso might fall from some unknown star and fish me out, lifting me up at the very moment before I touch the ground.

—Isolde, this is the conduct of a perfect man.

The wind rocks me back and forth. Below, the gaze of men tethers me to their earthly fear on a sad plain with a lone house visible in the distance and a plume of smoke that tries to lift it to the sky.

The house where the crime took place can never be freed from its little patch of land. And yet, although the spectacle has now become rather dismal, the night is brighter than ever; there is no seat to spare in all the heavens. And all this to see what?

The beautiful woman's throat takes the form of a song.

And she will sing, she will sing, certain that I am not about to die. She will sing despite the season's waning, despite the night rolling down from the mountains, despite the difficult terrain. She will sing.

And the child will stop crying over his little white boat. And the finest of stars will appear above his head, deep in the recess, beyond his delicate pillows, on the true reefs of his final dream.

Perhaps we will hear the confused voice in a vast song because the sea is spread out over several player-pianos and occasionally surrenders to its own instincts.

Then comes the hour of transfiguration. The sea sweats and writhes in intimate pain. Each wave turns into an angel and flies away.

Woe unto him who dared raise a hand against the sea!

You do not know this and so I tell you now: by night, when no-one is watching, the sea turns into a great monument and they say that at its peak there stands a solemn statue of itself.

No-one will ever know the truth of it, nor the number of mistakes that each man makes at every moment of his life.

Upon how many errors do mankind's inventions rest?

Those inventions finer than an electric spark, or a woman's legs. Here all wise men bow, here prophets kneel, here the cock crows and where its song ends a landscape is born, as you all know. Afterwards only the hands of castaways can be seen clinging to the waves, and a bottle that floats away to tell their tale of so much distress.

Isolde, if only you knew!

The sky has changed seven times. And it will change again because of the sea. Because the sea has turned into a balloon, slipped its moorings and drifted away into the sky.

¿Qué sacáis con apuntar vuestros cañones y con tocar las campanas?

En el horizonte, el sol que se pone, extiende la mano y nos mira apenas detrás de sus cinco dedos separados como los rayos de una rueda. ¿Qué podemos hacer?

Sobre el campo desierto cae el huevo de un águila que pasaba volando sin saber a dónde dirigir sus pasos. Ese será el campo de la fecundidad durante algunos años y acaso allí mismo nazca una gran capital.

Los telescopios se levantan y se pierden en la eternidad. El cielo se desnuda. Cruzan aerolitos y relámpagos más allá de la Vía Láctea, pasa el cortejo ceremonioso de los cometas y nadie teme ya la cólera de Dios.

El cielo se desnuda y se ven los ojos agonizantes del que todo lo creó.

El cielo se desnuda y se ve el fantasma nocturno que lleva a los astros el alimento cotidiano.

El cielo se desnuda y se ve la gruta de candelabros en cuyo centro duerme la mujer de carne que todos conocemos envuelta en sus cabellos.

Pasan las cebras sonámbulas al galope y se ven las ventanas que se abren en la oscuridad como parásitos pegadas a la noche.

¡Ah, si tú supieras! Yo estoy escondido adentro de tu sombra. Yo soy el árbol recién nacido adentro de tus ojos. Soy el niño de pies desnudos como estatua que grita en el naufragio entre los reflejos impasibles.

Soy el espectro que se aleja guiado por sus palomas, esas palomas llenas de sabiduría que se nutren de la luz de los faroles titubeantes.

Heme aquí fatigado y terrible, más terrible que el barco desahuciado que se aleja aullando por el cielo y muere dulcemente como un hombre o como un perro cuando siente por primera vez el peso de su esqueleto debajo de la carne.

¡Ah, si tú vieras! Cuando se abre el vientre materno como una jaula y la mujer levanta los brazos al infinito ofreciendo todos los vuelos futuros.

Si tú vieras. Los tejados temblorosos antes de levantarse para siempre. Los tejados que se irán quién sabe a dónde con su carga de nubes.

Si tú vieras ahora el insecto que salta al contacto de dos cables vengativos y puede tomar hasta forma de hombre para el ojo que mira con atención.

Y la inconsciencia de la noche rodeada por un canal profundo; la inconsciencia de los árboles que se baten frecuentemente. Cuántas veces los he visto tirarse del pelo e insultarse por un pájaro.

What use is there in aiming your cannons and ringing your bells?

On the horizon, the setting sun reaches out a hand and barely looks at us from just behind its five fingers, separated like the spokes of a wheel. What can we do?

Above the deserted countryside an egg falls from a passing eagle, that was unsure of its destination. This will be a fertile field for years to come and perhaps a great capital will arise there.

Telescopes are raised and become lost in eternity. The sky strips off. Meteorites and lightning-flashes cross beyond the Milky Way, the ceremonial procession of comets passes by and no-one fears the wrath of God any more.

The sky strips off and the dying eyes of the creator of all things can be seen.

The sky strips off and the nocturnal ghost that brings daily refreshments to the stars is revealed.

The sky strips off and the cavern of candelabras appears; in its centre sleeps the woman of flesh that we all know, wrapped in her tresses.

Zebras gallop by in their sleep and windows can be seen that open onto the darkness, clinging to the night like parasites.

Ah, if only you knew! I am hidden inside your shadow. I am the newborn tree inside your eyes. I am the child barefoot as a statue calling out from the shipwreck amidst the impassive reflections.

I am the spectre that leaves, guided by its doves, those doves full of wisdom that feed off the light from flickering streetlamps.

I have grown exhausted here, and terrible, more terrible than the doomed ship that goes howling through the sky and dies quietly like a man or a dog feeling for the first time the weight of the skeleton beneath its flesh.

Ah, if you could see it! When the maternal womb opens like a cage and the woman raises her arms to infinity offering all flights to come.

If you could see it. The trembling roofs before they rise up forever. The roofs that will leave for who knows where, laden with clouds.

If you could see now the insect that jumps at the contact of two vindictive cables and might assume the form of a man, as far as the attentive observer can tell.

And the unconsciousness of night surrounded by a deep channel; the unconsciousness of trees that so often clash. How many times have I seen them tug at each other's hair and hurl insults over a bird.

Ante tales misterios, ante tales fuerzas ocultas, la inconsciencia del mar, que podría de repente partirse por la mitad, es algo increíble.

Pero tú sabes que llegará el día en que serán tocados por la gracia como las montañas y entonces cada uno tendrá una aureola en torno.

Entonces veremos a las niñas que salen del colegio, en un vuele liviano con las trenzas al viento hacia el volantín que las aguarda a la entrada del volcán.

Veremos la estatua que se pasea sobre las casas, lavada por la lluvia como las heridas del guerrero. Veremos las transformaciones del silencio y los éxtasis del que contempla los juegos del ocaso y luego la estrella parpadeando en la corriente de aire.

Mas sólo el hombre que agoniza verá una flor agitando las manos adentro del vientre de la mujer amada. Y después se beberá la muerte de un sorbo.

La mujer podrá alejarse barriendo la vida con sus faldas, podrá esperar desnuda encima de la noche, con toda su hermosura en libertad.

El la podrá asomarse al balcón de su belleza, podrá pasearse con su espalda blanca llena de nocturnos sin importarle que la lluvia caiga sobre sus huesos, la lluvia donde raras veces pueden colgarse los ahorcados. Pero ella huele la tristeza, oye la voz de las tumbas y abre la boca para morder la muerte.

El hombre que se acerca tiene atados los ojos y levanta un himno o una planta acuática en la mano.

Todos los puentes se derrumban y la reina no puede pasar, la reina con el cerebro perfumado por sus pensamientos, la reina con los ojos azules olientes a mar.

Por sus poros escapa la fiebre y sus cinco sentidos se mueren a la puerta misma del misterio.

Sólo el seno del corazón sigue viviendo, rodeado de sus vasallos, con todos sus mitos de estatua. Sigue viviendo y mirando, mirando como un ojo desorbitado, sin obedecer las órdenes del creador, que truena desde el fondo de su sueño.

¡Cuántos sacos de oro amontona el avaro en su caverna para comprar ese seno que flotará hasta el fin de los siglos en su barrica llena de recuerdos!

Acaso un niño inexperto con los labios envenenados de quimeras va a morderlo ahora que tantas manos se tienden hacia él. Acaso va a librar una batalla encarnizada, fuera de sus años, por el sexo que se adivina, paseando bajo las ropas de sombra.

Before such mysteries, before such occult powers, the unconsciousness of the sea which could cleave in two at any moment is an incredible thing.

But you know the day will come when they will be touched by grace like the mountains and then each in turn will have a halo.

Then we shall see the girls as they come out of school, flying lightly with their braids in the wind towards the kite that awaits them at the entrance to the volcano.

We will see the statue wandering over the houses, washed by rain like a warrior's wounds. We will see the transformations of silence and the ecstasy of those watching the sunset play and then the star twinkling in the breeze.

But only a dying man will see a flower waving its hands inside the womb of the beloved woman. And afterwards he will drink death down in one gulp.

The woman might walk away, sweeping life aside with her skirts; she might wait, naked above the night, all her beauty set free.

She might lean over the balcony of her beauty, walk around with her white back full of evening stars, not bothered by the rain falling on her bones, the rain where hanged men can seldom be strung up. But she scents sadness, she hears the voice of the grave and opens her mouth to bite into death.

The man approaching is blindfolded and raises a hymn or an aquatic plant in his hand.

All the bridges collapse and the queen cannot pass, the queen whose mind is perfumed by her thoughts, the queen with blue eyes smelling of the sea.

Fever escapes through her pores and her five senses perish at the very threshold of mystery.

Only the heart's breast keeps on living, surrounded by its vassals, with all their myths concerning statues. It keeps on living and watching, watching like a bulging eye, disobeying the orders of its Creator, who thunders from the depths of his dreams.

How many sacks of gold does the miser hoard in his cavern to buy that breast, which will float until the end of time in his barrel of memories!

Perhaps a clumsy child, lips poisoned by chimeras, will bite him, now that so many hands are extended this way. Perhaps, older than his years, he will fight a furious battle for the sex one can only guess at, beneath the shadow's garments.

El la es el fantasma de piel transparente que no tiene rostro, sino un vacío redondo entre el pelo y el cuello.

Huye, niño delicado, con tu corona de caricias en la cabeza. Huye, te digo, a las cavernas del polo y canta mientras la hermosa legendaria escucha el sonido de las balas que corren tras ella.

* * *

Tendida la red de seno a seno otras han podido esperar.

Durante la noche, el precioso temblor se esconde en las grutas marinas. Allí baja el buscador de perlas, y a veces ha encontrado tendida sobre las aguas a la joven legendaria con los brazos atados. Entonces vuelve a subir la escala que cuelga de la noche y se pierde en la zona de los pájaros agoreros.

Desde la más alta roca puede lanzar una cuerda a la mujer crucificada en sus despojos y levantarla hasta la cima de los árboles donde trepan angustiados los que llevan aún el recuerdo del diluvio.

Corred a secaros en la boca del volcán que pronto levantará sus banderas en señal de triunfo.

Niño terrestre, cuando tratas de conciliar las alas con tus ojos humedecidos, olvidas las florescencias del laberinto interno, olvidas la caverna luminosa de los poseídos.

El volcán sabrá recordarte lo que olvidas y te lanzará una flor a la memoria y entonces verás pasar ante ti todo el universo como el salvaje parado en la montaña mira pasar el huracán o el río lleno de árboles desgajados.

La mujer que todos conocemos se alejará de ti por la orilla de los astros errantes con la carga de su cabellera en las espaldas, se alejará bajo una luna que se hincha por glotonería o acaso por la lluvia periódica de las nieves eternas. Se alejará la mujer con un cadáver precioso bajo el brazo y verá venir hacia ella de pronto una isla de colores violentos.

Su cabellera augusta caerá sobre el mar entre las algas milenarias. Se vestirá de la locura con toda su luz propia y será como la pantalla de seda que mira el moribundo.

Entretanto, el otro, en su cárcel de sabiduría, no podrá levantar los ojos sin ver sobre cada libro, sobre cada microscopio la estatua de senos enormes y vientre pulido que anima su propio corazón.

She is the ghost with transparent skin who, instead of a face, has a circular void between hair and neck.

Flee, delicate child, with your crown of caresses on your head. Flee, I tell you, to the polar caverns and sing while the legendary beauty listens to the sound of bullets racing after her.

* * *

With the net extended from breast to breast, others could wait.

During the night, the sweet quake hides in undersea caverns. There the pearl-diver descends, and sometimes he has found there the legendary maiden lying upon the waters, her arms bound. Then he climbs back up the ladder suspended from the night and vanishes into the region where there are birds of augury.

From the highest rock he can toss a rope to the woman crucified amongst her plunder and lift her to the treetops, where all those who still bear memories of the Flood climb anxiously.

Run and dry yourselves at the mouth of the volcano which will soon raise its banners in triumph.

Earthly child, when you try to reconcile wings with your moist eyes, you forget the flowering of the inner labyrinth, you forget the luminous cavern of the possessed.

The volcano can remind you of whatever you forget and will throw you a flower in its memory, then you will see the whole universe pass before you, just as the savage standing on the mountain watches the hurricane or the river full of uprooted trees pass by.

The woman we all know will drift away from you along the shores of wandering stars, with the weight of her hair on her shoulders, drift away under a moon swollen by gluttony or perhaps by the occasional rain of eternal snows. The woman will drift away with a handsome corpse under her arm and she will suddenly see an island of violent colours coming towards her.

Her majestic hair will fall into the sea amidst the age-old seaweed. She will be clothed in madness, glowing with her own light, and will be like a silk screen watched by a dying man.

Meanwhile, the other, in his prisoned of learning, will not be able to raise his eyes without seeing on every book, on every microscope, the statue with enormous breasts and a polished belly, bringing his own heart to life.

Esa es la estatua del alcohol vivo que brota de sus poros y cae en cascada hasta los pies encadenados.

Y ese juego que habéis creído que es el juego de la vida, no es sino el juego de la muerte.

He ahí al hombre sobre la mujer desde el principio del mundo hasta el fin del mundo. El hombre sobre la mujer eternamente como la piedra encima de la tumba.

No otra cosa sois que la muerte sobre la muerte. Contempla el gesto de espasmo de aquella que se muere en la muerte.

Así, pues, atraviesas la vida encerrada adentro de la muerte.

—Isolda, en vano suspiras en la noche, en vano gritas mi nombre cuando ya no oigo, cuando un sudor de sangre me cubre las orejas, cuando el cielo se vacía en mi retina. Todo hombre es un cobarde. No creas en los excepcionales que te pinta el sueño caído de otros astros menos palpables. El místico es el hombre del pavor, es el hombre que no quiere estar solo, es el que quiere ser dos por miedo a la soledad.

¡Ah, si tú supieras!

Qué no daría yo por hacerles callar con su voz azulada y romperles las formas y los colores del sentimiento eterno o pasajero, siempre dulce, demasiado dulce para el paladar de un náufrago infinito.

Los acontecimientos están por encima de la voz humana. El fenómeno que se condensa ahora en una bandera de mármol es mucho más importante que tus artes, tus artificios y tus artimañas.

El papel de música es un almacigo sin destino. No brotarán de allí las selvas futuras, míralo y verás que apenas marca un viñedo momentáneo.

El mar te trae el ataúd sensible hasta la puerta de tu casa, acaso hasta el mismo borde de tu cama, para que te encierres en él con tu preciosa histeria y con tus alaridos, esos alaridos sucios, sucios como las lágrimas de la demostración algebraica del dolor.

Enciérrate en él y que no salga la semilla de tu vientre, que podría ser un piano con sus microbios de crepúsculo, un piano de alma turbulenta que salta como agua hirviente.

Levanta los brazos, mujer, y pide perdón a la criatura que se mece entre tus piernas y no quiere saber nada de la luz de tus pequeños faroles domésticos.

Sopla, sopla y apaga esas luces de quimera con una palabra mágica.

This is the statue with living alcohol gushing from its pores and cascading down to its shackled feet.

And this game you believed was the game of life is nothing but the game of death.

Here is man on top of woman from the beginning of the world, until the end of the world. Man on top of woman forever like the stone over the tomb.

You are none other than death on top of death. Consider the gestures, the spasms of that woman who is dying in death.

So, you pass through life locked inside death.

—Isolde, in vain do you sigh at night, in vain do you cry out my name when I can no longer hear, when a bloody sweat covers my ears, when the sky empties into my retina. Every man is a coward. Do not believe in the exceptional things that your dream, fallen from less tangible stars, paints for you. The mystic is a man of dread, a man who does not want to be alone, the one who, from fear of loneliness, wishes he were two.

Ah, if only you knew!

What I would not give to silence them with their bluish voices and break the forms and colours of their eternal or fleeting feelings, always sweet, too sweet for the palate of an infinite castaway.

Events rank higher than the human voice. The phenomenon now condensed into a marble banner is much more important than your arts, your artifices, or your artfulness.

Sheet music is a seedbed with no destiny. No future forests will grow there, look at it and you will see that it barely marks out a temporary vineyard.

The sea brings the sensitive coffin to your house door, perhaps to your bedside, so that you can shut yourself in it with your sweet hysteria and your cries, those filthy cries, filthy as the tears of the algebraic proof of pain.

Shut yourself inside it so that the seed cannot escape your womb, for it could be a piano with its twilight microbes, a piano with a turbulent soul jumping like boiling water.

Raise your arms, woman, and beg forgiveness of the creature that is cradled between your legs and wants nothing to do with the light from your household lanterns.

Blow, blow and extinguish those illusory lights with one magic word.

Sopla y apaga la estatua que ya va a preguntar el camino, que ya quiere saber el tiempo que hará mañana.

Baja el dedo con que ibas a señalar el destino ofrecido, tus experiencias de sombra, mientras un barco está naufragando y salta de tromba en tromba, de abismo en abismo bajo el cielo negro.

Emplea mejor tu tiempo en ondular tus cabellos como un mar sencillo que escucha sus pájaros blandos al cruzar la tarde.

Guarda para la muchedumbre en fiesta hueca, acodada en las barandas del puerto tus lecciones nocturnas. Guarda para el la el ceremonial de tus senos, que ya no pueden tenerse en sí.

Luego ha de llevarte la carroza del rey con tu vientre y tus piernas, con tu mirada de cometa a través del gentío que te aplaude. ¿Qué más quieres?

El palacio tiene escalinatas que no se sabe dónde terminan, las columnas sostienen ojivas de planeta a planeta y en todos los jarrones hay cabezas cortadas.

A través de las rejas se ve la eternidad dormida con una placidez indescriptible. ¿Qué más quieres?

Ese es tu destino. Deja a cada cual su libertad que está al principio o al final del vuelo como una rama o un puerto. Y ahora calla.

El moribundo aprieta los labios para que no huya el pájaro definitivo a cantar su romanza sobre otras rocas.

Todo obedece a la cadencia de una voz que nadie sabe de dónde cae.

He ahí el destino de la mariposa magnética.

He ahí el esqueleto aguardando pacientemente su hora, escondido en las sombras. El esqueleto final que jugará al ajedrez bajo su casa de tierra, mientras viven sus sombreros en las calles ajenas.

Y podéis llorar porque semejante es el horóscopo del árbol.

Esconded las caricias en las cavernas de los pájaros polares en donde el hombre se clava estalactitas en los ojos y la mujer corre saltando entre los icebergs.

—Isolda, ya viene el huracán asolando el cementerio de las miradas, ya viene el huracán con la velocidad de los planetas lanzados al destino.

Escondámonos en las más hondas catacumbas y allí grabemos nuestro nombre en las piedras sensibles junto al nicho en donde debemos acostarnos por la eternidad.

Blow and extinguish the statue that is about to ask directions, that already wants to know how the weather will be tomorrow.

Lower the finger with which you were going to point to the destiny on offer, to your experiences of shadow, while a ship is sinking and jumping from tornado to tornado, from abyss to abyss beneath the black sky.

Better to use your time rippling your hair like a simple sea that listens to its timid birds as they pass through the evening.

Keep your night-time lectures for the hollow celebration of the crowd leaning on the harbour railings. Keep for them the ritual of your breasts that can no longer be hold up.

Soon the king's coach must carry you off with your womb and your legs, your cometary gaze, through the applauding crowd. What more do you want?

The palace has grand staircases that lead who knows where, columns that support arches from planet to planet and in every vase there are severed heads.

Through the bars eternity can be seen sleeping in indescribable serenity. What more do you want?

This is your destiny. Leave each to their own freedom which lies at the beginning or the end of the flight, like a shelter or a harbour. And now keep quiet.

The dying man purses his lips so that the last bird cannot escape to sing its song on other rocks.

Everything obeys the cadence of a voice that falls from who knows where.

This is the destiny of a magnetic butterfly.

This is the skeleton patiently awaiting its time, hidden in the shadows. The final skeleton that will play chess beneath its earthly house, while its hats live in the street outside.

And you might weep because such is the tree's horoscope.

Hide your caresses in the caverns of polar birds where men drive stalactites into their eyes and women run, leaping between icebergs.

—Isolde, the hurricane is already here, laying waste the cemetery of gazes, the hurricane is already here with the speed of planets hurled to their fate.

Let us hide in the deepest catacombs and carve our names there in the soft stone by the niche where we are to lie for eternity.

Allí los curiosos de mañana encontrarán nuestras calaveras y nuestros huesos mezclados.

Sangra la frente del Tiempo en la oscuridad sin reposo de la noche, sangra destrozada por montañas de espinas.

¡Qué importa!

En la terraza de la última cima mi garganta estuvo tragándose todos los truenos del cielo y mis dedos acariciaron el lomo de los relámpagos, mientras el sol detrás de la noche rehacía sus huestes y se preparaba para el ataque del día siguiente.

¿Oyes el ruido de las olas que se estrellan a causa de la oscuridad?

No temas. Vámonos. Es el velero de la muerte. El monstruo amado se acerca y viene a lamer nuestras manos.

La tierra es dulce y blanda como el colchón de la eternidad.

La esposa nos invita a la fiesta de sus entrañas. Su beso tiene gusto a labios de infinito y ha de llevarnos más lejos de lo que nadie puede sospechar.

Ahora pasas y yo veo adentro de tu corazón iluminado las arborescencias geológicas que marcan tu edad sobre la tierra.

¿Oyes el ruido de las olas que se estrellan en la noche? ¿Oyes el ruido de las olas que se rompen la cabeza?

Ahora pasas y te pierdes en los paisajes ayer inexpugnables, te vas por los caminos aún vivos y tan equívocos como siempre.

Ya te encontrarás al fantasma que grita: Sálvese el que pueda, y arroja sus sentimientos y sus recuerdos por la borda para hacerse más liviano.

Te encontrarás también al que bota sus años como el lastre de un globo y luego canta su inconsciencia con una voz de novio encadenado y satisfecho.

Te encontrarás al hombre que todo lo sabe, el hombre entristecido que nada ignora, que siempre tiene una respuesta pronta, la palabra madura en la rama de los labios, el hombre que ha estudiado las entrañas de la flor, que conoce el pasado, el presente y el futuro y la genealogía de cada ola.

A pesar de todo, el Misterio se presentará vestido con sus trajes de lujo. La alegría delicada de sus senos palpitantes o el dolor de sus ojos que sólo quieren libertarse, no han de temer a semejantes rivales.

Mujer, mira mis ojos, estos ojos condenados a cadena perpetua.

Y piensa que yo podría entrar en Dios como el buzo en el mar.

There the curious of tomorrow will find our skulls and our bones entwined.

Time's brow bleeds in the restless darkness of night, bleeds, torn apart by mountains of thorns.

What does it matter!

On the terrace of the highest peak my throat swallowed all the thunder from the sky, and my fingers stroked the lightning's back, while the sun regrouped its forces behind the night and prepared for the next day's attack.

Do you hear the sound of waves colliding because of the darkness?

Do not fear. Let us go. It is death's sailing ship. The beloved monster comes closer and licks at our hands.

The earth is gentle and soft as the mattress of eternity.

The bride invites us to the celebration of her womb. Her kiss tastes of infinity's lips and she has to carry us further than anyone could have thought possible.

Now you pass by and I see the geological tree-like forms inside your glowing heart that mark your age on earth.

Do you hear the sound of waves colliding in the night? Do you hear the sound of waves banging their heads together?

Now you pass by and are lost in landscapes that were impregnable yesterday, you travel roads that are still alive but as ambiguous as ever.

Soon you will encounter the ghost that cries out, Every man for himself, and flings its feelings and memories overboard so as to lighten the load.

You will encounter someone who discards his years like ballast from a balloon and then sings of his folly with the voice of a shackled and satisfied bridegroom.

You will encounter the man who knows everything, the grieving man who is aware of everything, who always has a ready answer, ripe words on the boughs of his lips, the man who has studied the flower's innards, who knows the past, the present and the future and the genealogy of every wave.

Despite of all this, the Mystery will appear dressed in lavish garments. The delicate joy of its heaving breast or the pain in its eyes that long only liberation, have no reason to fear such rivals.

Woman, look into my eyes, these eyes condemned to perpetual chains.

And consider that I could enter God as a diver does the sea.

Pero no hay un Dios suficientemente profundo para mi corazón, para la angustia de este corazón habituado a las más grandes olas y el corazón prefiere vegetar en su puerto y pudrirse entre las algas.

No creas que tengo miedo.

Ni un temblor me sacude cuando se abren grandes mis ojos y ven lo que se ve en el momento de morir. Porque yo he visto lo que vosotros sólo veréis entonces.

No tengo miedo. Sólo me estremezco cuando a veces encuentro mi voz en un hombre de antaño.

—Isolda, mírame en la batalla, mírame en el instante más desesperado, cuando todo está perdido. Entonces, sí, soy yo y seguramente me veo más hermoso que un buque luchando a muerte contra el mar.

Así digo y me preparo a ser raíz, mientras la tierra huye bramando por el cielo … Mientras la luna mira de reojo y el aire pierde sus límites propios.

¿Qué hacéis allí vosotros vestidos de negro? Estáis a la puerta de mi casa esperando mi entierro con coronas y laureles de fiesta. ¿Y si yo ordeno que mi cadáver se arroje a los perros?

* * *

Todo peso es inútil y el recuerdo sólo entorpece la marcha y dobla las espaldas.

Cuelgan de nuestros cuellos tanto brazos y senos y ojos de vírgenes legendarias que nuestros labios toman forma de flor obsesionada.

Es forzoso el crimen si queréis volar otra vez. Un rítmico asesinato de gimnasta o el malabarismo del prestidigitador que sabe apagar las llamaradas en el vientre o cambiarlas de sitio en el minuto preciso, haciéndolas surgir en el violín del más descuidado. De allí subirán en escala delicadas hasta las últimas cimas.

Envuelto en lazos de fuego el que pueda danzar será el preferido y sólo él sabrá envolver a la joven legendaria en espirales de serpiente. Allí quedará embrujada hasta el fin de los siglos.

Y habéis de saber que el peso del alarido no podrá romper los círculos luminosos cuando llegue la macabra estación y se vea el desfile de los espectros hacia el polo.

But there is no God deep enough for my heart, for the anguish of this heart grown used to the biggest waves and so my heart prefers to vegetate in its harbour, to rot amongst the seaweed.

Do not think I am afraid.

Not even a quake shakes me when my eyes open wide and see what can be seen at the moment of death. For I have seen what you will only see then.

I am not afraid. The only time I shudder is when I encounter my own voice in a man from the past.

—Isolde, watch me in battle, watch me at the most desperate moment, when all is lost. Then, yes, that truly is me, and I surely look finer than a ship in a death struggle with the sea.

That's what I say and I prepare to become a root, while the earth flees bellowing through the heavens … While the moon glances out of the corner of its eye, and the air loses its own boundaries.

What are you doing there, all dressed in black? You stand at the door of my house awaiting my funeral with wreaths and festive laurels. And what if I order my corpse to be thrown to the dogs?

* * *

Every weight is useless and memory only hinders progress and bends backs.

Hanging from our necks are so many arms, breasts and eyes of legendary virgins that our lips take on the form of obsessed flowers.

Crime is unavoidable if you wish to fly again. A gymnast's rhythmic murder or the sleight of hand of a conjurer who knows how to extinguish flames in the womb or shift them at just the right moment, making them emerge from the violin of the most distracted man. From there they will delicately climb ladders to the very top.

Wrapped with bonds of fire, whoever can dance will be chosen and only he will know how to bind the legendary maiden with serpentine coils. There she will remain enchanted until the end of time.

And you have to know the weight of a scream will not suffice to break any glowing circles when the grim season arrives and the procession of spectres can be seen all the way to the Pole.

Después vendrá la fiesta de las madres y la fiesta de las novias paradas arriba de la torre con los ojos llenos de ceremonias íntimas, los ojos abiertos para que nazcan cómodamente los cuatro puntos cardinales, que luego crecen sin medida y desbordan del mundo.

¡Ah, si tú supieras! Las manos del soliloquio se levantan hasta la frente y hacen toldo a los ojos para mirar más lejos.

¿Todo esto para qué? Pronto vendrán las lágrimas y una muerte a escoger en la variedad seleccionada por los siglos.

¿Oyes clavar el ataúd nocturno?¿Ves a la hermosa desnuda en su acuario de muerte?

La circunferencia del suspiro en donde creímos sepultar todo aquel pasado puede poblarse de una vegetación tropical y de una fauna vertiginosa.

Crecerán flores debajo del acuario, crecerán flores debajo de las tierras del cementerio y un día aparecerá sobre la tierra el ataúd más viejo levantado en brazos de olores como tallos robustos.

—Isolda, el peso de las lágrimas no puede romper el mármol. Pero he ahí lo que hizo el milagro de la memoria musculosa.

¿Oyes clavar el ataúd nocturno?

Tú eres el cabal lo que monta la noche para sus más largas marchas.

Sin embargo, nunca llegarás al fin. Recorrerás toda la historia de los hombres y no encontrarás lo que buscabas.

La cultura física de los sepultureros hace liviano el mundo y soportable el espectáculo. Sabemos que la lluvia de tierra será eterna, sabemos que el otoño será una fuente de hojas siempre viva, una cascada interminable entre las ramas. Sabemos que el invierno alargará su polo a nuestros ojos cuando los juegos de agua se convierten en estatuas en medio de las llanuras más blancas de la luna. Sabemos que allá lejos al borde del invierno se verán los ojos de la que aguarda en vano y olvidó que la culpa era suya o por lo menos debía partirse en dos mitades semejantes.

Volará el invierno agitando sus alas pesadas de quién sabe qué metal desconocido y ello sólo porque tú supiste pedir perdón.

Volverán a cruzar las caravanas legendarias que no tienen más título de nobleza que su propia antigüedad, su experiencia indiscutible semejante a las pirámides o al sillón del mandarín que ha oído pasar la música de tantos siglos sin destino aparente a su mirada porque ella estaba siempre fija en los senos desnudos de la bella torturada que se retuerce tendida sobre las planchas infernales.

Afterwards comes the festival of mothers and the festival of brides standing atop the tower, their eyes full of intimate rituals, their eyes open so that the four cardinal points can comfortably be born, and then grow unrestrained and flood the world.

Ah if only you knew! The soliloquist's hands rise to his brow making a shade so his eyes might see further.

All this for what? Soon there will be tears, and a death to choose from amongst the range selected by the ages.

Do you hear night's coffin being nailed shut? Do you see the naked beauty in her aquarium of death?

The circumference of the sigh, where we thought all the past could be buried, may yet be stocked with tropical vegetation and teeming wildlife.

Flowers will grow beneath the aquarium, flowers will grow beneath the cemetery soil and one day the oldest coffin will appear on the ground, raised on arms of fragrance like sturdy saplings.

—Isolde, the weight of your tears cannot break marble. But here is what the miracle of muscle memory once wrought.

Do you hear night's coffin being nailed shut?

You are the stallion that night mounts for its longest journeys.

But you will never reach the end. You will rove across all of mankind's history and never find what you seek.

The fitness of gravediggers makes the world lighter and the spectacle bearable. We know that rain will last forever on earth, we know that Autumn will be an ever-living source of leaves, an endless cascade amongst the branches. We know that Winter will extend its pole as far as our eyes when fountains turn into statues on the moon's whitest plains. We know that far away, at the edge of Winter, the eyes of the woman can be seen who waits in vain, one who forgot that the fault was all hers or should at least be divided into two equal halves.

Winter will beat its heavy wings of some unknown metal, because you knew how to beg forgiveness.

The legendary caravans that possess no titles of nobility other than their own antiquity, will take to the roads once more, their incontrovertible experience similar to the pyramids or to the armchair of the mandarin who has heard the music of so many centuries pass by, with no destination apparent to his gaze because it was always fixed on the bare breasts of a tortured beauty, writhing, lying on infernal plates.

A veces antes del fin deseado aparece el hospital abierto y ordenado en su blancura como un restaurante con sus mesas que esperan la igualdad del sentimiento.

Parte el tren inesperado a la satisfacción de sus deseos. En todas partes aguarda anhelante el fusil en la mano temblorosa.

A veces la emboscada camina hacia nosotros, a veces se aleja en otras direcciones y parece no habernos visto o bien habernos olvidado.

A veces el ladrón huye llevando la mano y los senos cortados de la hermosa legendaria en sus bolsillos, otras veces huye el doctor con la valija en donde escondió los ojos de la amada inolvidable.

El camino sigue derecho y sólo se corta en el mar. Allí están las barcas aguardando apoyadas en la baranda del crepúsculo. En el momento del partir definitivo vuelve a aparecer la joven viajera con la cabeza rodeada de siete arcos iris, arrastrando a su marcha el coro de suplicantes que se nutren de su aliento precioso.

Ella quiere que todos vivan preocupados de sus ojos comunicantes, de su cuello rodeado de encajes melodiosos, de sus espaldas rodeadas de pieles magnéticas y de su sombrero de arco iris.

Ella, cuando ve nuestros ojos agujereados por la luz, se asusta, sus huesos tiemblan debajo de la carne preparada a las catástrofes.

Los instrumentos de tortura son todos semejantes en la base interna de su razón de ser. Hasta las palomas que vuelan de cielo en cielo saben esto desde su más tierna infancia.

La bella legendaria encadenada a sus senos vive en la inocencia de sus cabellos volátiles. Nunca ha mirado a la golondrina desesperada en su bocal de aire, ni otros pájaros semejantes que quieren romper la atmósfera terrestre y huir para siempre de nuestro lado.

Inclina su cabeza bajo los tatuajes del cielo y nada ve. Apenas podría decirse que siente las cadenas de su vientre.

¿Y esto sabéis por qué? Porque no falta alguna muerta despedazada por los puñales del fantasma escondido detrás de sus cortinas, que haga al fin el gesto de rechazar y de volver el rostro con naturalidad.

Todas las novias duermen en el mismo lecho.

Allí están durmiendo cruzadas por el mismo sueño con los ojos acuáticos nadando entre las mismas algas submarinas. Desde el principio del mundo las hojas de la virginidad van cayendo fuera de su otoño propio, sin razón ninguna.

Sometimes, before the desired conclusion, the hospital appears, open and tidy in its whiteness, like a restaurant with tables awaiting the equality of feeling.

The unexpected train departs for the satisfaction of its desires. Everywhere rifles wait eagerly in trembling hands.

Sometimes the ambush comes towards us, sometimes it goes off in other directions, seeming not to have seen us or simply to have forgotten us.

Sometimes it is the thief fleeing, with the severed hand and breasts of the legendary beauty in his pockets, at other times it is the doctor fleeing with his Gladstone bag where he hid the eyes of the unforgettable beloved.

The road goes straight on and stops only at the sea. There, boats are waiting, leaning on the railings of dusk. At the exact moment of departure the young traveller reappears with her head swathed in seven rainbows, dragging along a chorus of supplicants that feed on her sweet breath.

She wants everyone to live preoccupied by her expressive eyes, her neck swathed in melodious lace, her shoulders swathed in magnetic furs and her rainbow-coloured hat.

When she sees our eyes pierced by the light she is startled, her bones tremble beneath the flesh, prepared for catastrophe.

All instruments of torture are the same in their innermost raison d'être. Even the doves that fly from sky to sky have known this since their earliest infancy.

The legendary beauty shackled to her own breasts lives in the innocence of her volatile hair. Never has she looked upon the desperate swallow in its jar of air, nor upon other, similar birds that also wish to break through the earth's atmosphere and flee forever from our side.

She bends her head beneath the sky's tattoos and sees nothing. It could scarcely be said she even senses the chains around her womb.

And do you know why? Because there is never a shortage of dead women cut to pieces by the daggers of the ghost hidden behind her curtains, who in the end makes a gesture of refusal and turns his face away quite naturally.

All brides sleep in the same bed.

There they are, asleep, visited by the same dream, their aquatic eyes swimming amongst the same underwater seaweed. Since the beginning of the world the leaves of virginity have continued to fall outside their own Autumn, for no reason whatsoever.

La lámpara que vela es semejante a una medusa con los ojos heridos. Y ellas no comprenden.

En la ventana abierta la mano del esqueleto tiende los dedos para atraer los pájaros perdidos sin remedio a causa de sus impulsos migratorios o de los imanes de la selva. Y ellas no comprenden.

Mueren los pájaros atragantados por su propio instrumento musical, ese instrumento a cuyo son acompasado crecen nuestras vértebras y asciende la savia hasta la cima del cerebro para alimentar las luminarias a la presión debida. Y ellas no comprenden.

Afuera las multitudes se amontonan y se disputan ferozmente los peldaños del santuario milagroso. Suben de rodillas por las escalas de sus himnos y tratan de besar las garras del dragón convulsionado.

El capitán de los lirios defiende los derechos de su casta y seguirá perfumando, mientras viva y el triunfo sea suyo. En cambio, la mujer desnuda es arrojada a golpes desde arriba y va azotando sus senos en los peldaños donde se quiebran sus lamentos.

Así un día caerá de improviso en la sala del consejo cuando el rey discute con sus favoritos. Ella será la llave del misterio, porque la verdad escapa con la sangre de sus heridas.

Allí está la luz, la luz que los monjes no quisieron ver, preocupados sólo de recoger todo el maná posible y responder a los saludos del dragón.

Cegados por los relámpagos del Dios que estaban adorando, quedaron convertidos en estatua. Ese debía ser su triste fin porque la esfinge no paga las visitas y ni siquiera abre los ojos para mirar el cataclismo.

Huye de aquí. Atraviesa el río inmenso con la corneja al hombro, el río que pasa como un tren y sigue su marcha hasta el infinito.

Atraviesa el río que corre entre palmeras y cigüeñas, palmeras más grandes que los ojos de la amada, el río que no conoces, ese que te señalo, ese que en la noche se llena de linternas mágicas y se duerme bajo su toldo propio si la pastora impasible sabe cantarle junto al oído.

—Isolda, ¿cuál es tu voz y cuál debiera ser? ¿En dónde está tu voz y en dónde debiera estar?

Harás un arpa de las ramas y espantarás a las abejas. Te quedarás sola en medio de los espectros que has sabido atraer con tus encantos. Tus dedos delicados arrancarán sus mejores melodías a las hojas temblantes y tus ojos, allá arriba, mirarán el mundo como la hostia en la custodia.

The lamp that keeps vigil resembles a jellyfish with injured eyes. And they do not understand.

At the open window the skeleton's hand extends its fingers to lure birds that are irretrievably lost because of their migratory impulses magnets in the forest. And they do not understand.

These birds die, suffocated by their own musical instrument, an instrument whose rhythmic sound causes vertebrae to grow and sap to rise to the summit of the brain, feeding the lights at their correct pressure. And they do not understand.

Outside crowds gather, arguing furiously on the steps of the miraculous sanctuary. On their knees they ascend the stairs of their hymns, attempting to kiss the claws of the twitching dragon.

The captain of the lilies defends the rights of his caste and will continue dispensing perfume as long as he lives and triumph is his. By contrast, the naked woman is hurled down by blows from above and strikes her breasts against the steps where her lamentations falter.

Thus one day she will unexpectedly fall into the council chamber while the king is in discussions with his favourites. She will be the key to the mystery, because truth will escape with the blood from her wounds.

There lies the light, light that the monks, concerned only with gathering as much manna as possible and replying to the dragon's greetings, do not care to see.

Blinded by lightning from the God they were worshipping, they remained, turned into statues. This ought to have been their sad end because the sphinx does not return visits, nor does it even open its eyes to witness the cataclysm.

Flee from here. Cross the immense river with a raven on your shoulder, the river that passes like a train and maintains its progress to infinity.

Cross the river that runs between the palm trees and storks, palms taller than the eyes of the beloved, the river you do not know, the one I point out to you, the one that, at night, fills with magic lanterns and falls asleep beneath its own canopy if the impassive shepherdess knows how to sing in its ear.

—Isolde, what is your voice and what should it be? Where is your voice and where should it be?

You will make a harp from the branches and you will scare away the bees. You will remain alone amongst the spectres you have been able to lure with your spells. Your delicate fingers will pick out the finest melodies from

No dejes que la luna te desnude, ni que te cuelguen de cualquiera estrella lo mismo que los ahorcados por hermosos delitos, los ahorcados que se columpian sobre la eternidad.

¡Qué te importa si el galán se arroja de la torre y pierde la vista en el camino!

Déjalo en paz. Dirás que sus ojos supieron morir con un sobrio heroísmo. No faltará quien recoja los cantos del galán volcánico, ni quien encienda una bujía en su memoria o ponga una corona amenazante en su cabeza de muerto, en donde sólo los ojos guardan aún una cierta vida y se levanta en puntillas todas las mañanas para ir a sembrar la agitación en tu pecho endurecido.

Cantas, ¡oh inconsciente!, mientras agonizan las serpientes de tus brazos como las bayaderas de los templos.

Las olas son lentas para morir.

¿Oyes clavar el ataúd del mar?

—Isolda, aquella otra también murió. El, el culpable, se aleja por el último camino acompañado de sus crímenes.

Todas murieron. Fueron desembarcando las estatuas en las diversas estaciones.

Con la sonrisa atada aquélla se quedó en medio de los campos.

Pero hay una, hay una que encalló en las arenas de mi memoria y se sustenta de mis células.

Un día volamos enlazados sobre las cimas efervescentes. Juntos rodamos al abismo ilimitado y allí elevamos las brujerías del sexo a un rito de naufragio sin defensa.

Cinco meses mi cabeza durmió sobre su vientre. Aquel nudo de arterias y de huesos hacía crujir nuestra fortuna desde el encuentro luminoso. Desde entonces vivo siguiendo su entierro.

Voy bajando la escala de su recuerdo que cada día se hace más larga y cada hora más propicia, entretejida por estrellas que le dieron toda su luz antes de morir, que se desangraron por ella sin esperar recompensa alguna.

—Isolda, a veces quisiera ahogarme en un océano de mujeres.

Reina la noche en las dos orillas de tu mirada y yo me paseo por el mundo, me paseo en silencio, me paseo semejante a la soledad de un muerto.

Me paseo por el mundo sin mirar el mundo, me paseo por el mundo sin oír el mundo, me paseo semejante a la dignidad de un muerto.

the trembling leaves and from up there your eyes will observe the world as if it were the host on display.

Do not let the moon undress you, do not let them hang you from some star like those men hanged for beautiful crimes, swinging over eternity.

What does it matter to you if your suitor throws himself from the tower and loses his sight along the way!

Leave him in peace. You will say that his eyes knew how to die with sober heroism. There will be no lack of those to gather up the volcanic suitor's songs, nor of those to light a candle in his memory, or place a menacing wreath upon his skull, where the eyes alone still retain some trace of life, rising on tiptoe every morning to sow turmoil in your hardened breast.

You sing, oh thoughtless one!, while your snake-like arms writhe like those of Hindu temple dancers.

The waves are slow to die.

Do you hear the sea's coffin being nailed shut?

—Isolde, that other woman also died. He, the guilty man, walk away down the final path accompanied by his crimes.

They all died. The statues were offloaded at various stops.

With a fixed smile, that woman remained in the middle of the fields.

But there is one, there is one washed up on my memory's sands, who feeds on my cells.

One day we flew bound together over effervescent peaks. Together we tumbled into the limitless abyss and there we elevated the sorceries of sex to a rite of defenceless shipwreck.

For five months my head slept on her belly. That knot of arteries and bones made our fortune creak from the moment of our luminous encounter. Ever since, I have gone on living following her burial.

I go down the stairway of her memory, which every day grows longer and every hour more auspicious, interwoven with stars that gave her all their light before dying, that bled for her, expecting no reward.

—Isolde, there are times I would like to drown in an ocean of women.

Night reigns on both shores of your gaze and I wander through the world, wander in silence, wander like the loneliness of a dead man.

I wander through the world without looking at the world, I wander through the world without hearing the world, I wander with the dignity of a dead man.

¿Oyes? Están clavando mi ataúd. ¿Oyes cómo clavan mi ataúd? ¿Cómo encierran la noche en mi ataúd, la noche que será mía hasta el fin de los siglos?

Soy lento, lento para morir.

No temo a la nada ni la temería aunque no tuviera la seguridad de seguir en mi eco, de seguir intangible rodando de eco en eco.

—Isolda, tú has de encontrarme aún varias veces en muchos caminos de la eternidad.

Y también me encontraréis algunos de vosotros llevando los ojos culpables, atados con esposas y forcejeando para romperlas.

Mirad el muerto que se levanta en alta mar. Oíd la voz del muerto que se yergue en su sudario de olas.

Mirad al muerto que se levanta en la cumbre de la montaña.

Oíd, oíd la voz de los muertos.

La gran voz de los abuelos, la negra voz que tiene su raíz en lo más profundo de la tierra y que demora años y siglos en llegar a la superficie y más años y más siglos en encontrar una garganta preparada.

La garganta poderosa que sea como una trompeta. La trompeta de las edades, la trompeta de todos los que han sufrido, de todos los que han temblado en sudores de sangre sobre el terror o el desaliento, la trompeta de todos los dolores, de todos los rencores, de todas las venganzas. La trompeta de raíces pavorosas.

Oíd, oíd la voz de las tinieblas. Por mi garganta la tiniebla vuelve a la luz.

Entrad a vuestra propia caverna vertiginosa, bajad sin cloro-formo a vuestras íntimas profundidades. La sangre tiene luz propia y los huesos despiden chispas a causa de un fósforo afiebrado semejante a un contacto eléctrico.

Señoras y señores: Hay un muerto que aplasta sus cabellos bajo la cabeza adentro de su ataúd. Vosotros tenéis hermosos dientes para decir hermosas palabras.

Señoras y señores: Hay un pájaro que se abre en pleno vuelo y nos arroja la eternidad. Nos arroja entre sangre y vísceras la eternidad como una inmunda promesa.

El pájaro adivinado por los astrónomos conoce todos los secretos.

Señoras y señores: Hay un muerto que está deviniendo esqueleto en su ataúd. Las emanaciones de la carne rasgan la madera y hacen oscilar las puertas de piedra.

Do you hear it? They are nailing my coffin shut. Do you hear how they nail my coffin shut? How they shut the night inside my coffin, the night that will be mine until the end of time?

I am slow, slow to die.

I do not fear the void, nor would I fear it even if I were not certain of surviving in my echo, surviving intangibly, rolling from echo to echo.

—Isolde, you will encounter me many times yet on many roads to eternity.

And some among you will also encounter me, carrying my guilty eyes, shackled, and struggling to break free.

Watch the dead man rising up from the open sea. Hear the voice of the dead man standing upright in his shroud of waves.

Watch the dead man rising on the mountain top.

Hear, hear the voice of the dead.

The great voice of our ancestors, the dark voice whose roots lie in the deepest parts of the earth and take years, centuries to reach the surface, and still more years and more centuries to find a throat that is ready for it.

A powerful throat that can be like a trumpet. The trumpet of the ages, the trumpet of all who have suffered, of all who have trembled and sweated blood in terror and despair, the trumpet of all sorrows, of all rancour, all vengeance. The trumpet with terrifying roots.

Hear, hear the voice of darkness. Through my throat the darkness returns to light.

Enter your own dizzying cavern, descend without chloroform into your innermost depths. Blood has its own light and bones spark with fevered phosphorous, like an electric contact.

Ladies and gentlemen, there is a dead man inside his coffin flattening the hair beneath his head. You have fine teeth, for uttering fine words.

Ladies and gentlemen: There is a bird splitting open in full flight and hurling eternity down upon us. Hurling eternity at us, along with blood and viscera like a foul promise.

The bird prophesied by astronomers knows all secrets.

Ladies and gentlemen, there is a dead man in his coffin, turning into a skeleton. The emanations from his flesh gouge the wood and make the stone doors sway.

Habéis oído crujir las puertas de la tumba y habéis pensado que a dos metros de profundidad hay una ciudad de esqueletos plácidos y calaveras mordedoras. Hay una ciudad de rostros de cera y manos de cera. El polvo secular de vuestros huesos endurece las noches y cae como el tiempo en vuestra clepsidra interna porque vuestra sombra tiene la forma de la noche y es una pequeña noche en marcha.

Estáis allí en esa interminable posición en que quedáis después de haber bebido el vaso de infinito que destila el vacío y que os convierte en ceniza respetable de antepasado inmemorial. De todas esas cenizas puede el azar hacer un astro nuevo.

Y yo os digo, queridos oyentes, que el esqueleto desgraciado que es vuestro huésped nunca verá la luz, pues pasará del ataúd de vuestra carne al ataúd del sepulcro. Así, lleváis un prisionero atado en vuestro calabozo vagabundo y sin piedad. Mala suerte es ésta de ir en hombros de esa armazón que ha de vengarse y que sólo acecha el momento favorable.

El prisionero tiene sed de temperatura como la hermana ardiente, siente delirios de cielo en sus adentros, quiere salir de ese atardecer constante, saltar en un graznido salvaje como el volcán salta del fondo de la tierra y no se detiene hasta que llega a la luz, como el espanto adivinatorio brota del pecho y sube hasta los labios y los ojos convertidos en llagas de silencio. Vuestros huesos, ebrios de soledad, sienten los rumores del rocío en la sangre y adivinan que ellos son la última música, el postrer silbato después del fin del mundo sólo semejante a la sirena de un barco naufragado que sonara de repente en el fondo del mar.

Y cuando los huesos, señoras y señores, rompan los lazos que los atan entre sí como las constelaciones, harán un ruido fabuloso, un ruido de catástrofe para los oídos afinados, más violento que aquél de las lejanías que se libertan y se alejan al galope. Tal es el ansia del prisionero evadido que hace aullar los caminos y que asusta al tiempo sin entrañas, al tiempo que hace gestos de universo.

Señoras y señores: La culebra de los naufragios se muerde la cola y se agranda, se agranda hasta el infinito.

Adentro de sus círculos estamos nosotros sorbidos por el abismo de la futura podredumbre, arrojando pus por nuestros ojos como espuma de playas. En tanto los paisajes internos sienten el vuelo de los árboles, nuestros oídos, antes de despegarse y caer como hojas, alcanzan a oír el torbellino de las espigas que se ahondan. No hay esperanza de reposo. En vano el esqueleto detrás de su vidrio toma la actitud hierática del que va a

You heard the tomb's doors creaking and thought that, two metres below, there lay a city of quiet skeletons and bare-toothed skulls. There is a city of waxen faces and waxen hands. The ancient dust from your bones hardens the nights and falls like time into your inner water-clock because your shadow takes the form of night, a little night in motion.

You are there in that endless position where you have remained since drinking the cup of infinity which distils the void and turns you into the respectable ashes of our immemorial ancestors. Out of these ashes chance may yet forge a new star.

And I tell you, dear listeners, that the unfortunate skeleton that is your guest will never see the light, for he will pass from the coffin of your flesh to that of the tomb. Thus you carry a shackled prisoner into your drifter's pitiless dungeon. It is bad luck to shoulder this framework that will one day take its revenge.

The prisoner thirsts for warmth like an excited sister, feels heavenly delirium within, wants to escape this constant dusk, leap cackling wildly as the volcano erupts from the bowels of the earth, stopping at nothing until it reaches the light, as the prophesied terror breaks through the breast and rises to the lips, to the eyes turned into wounds of silence. Your bones, drunk with solitude, sense the murmuring dew in the blood and suspect they are the final music, the dying hiss after the end of the world comparable only to the siren of a wrecked ship suddenly blaring out from the sea floor.

And, ladies and gentlemen, when the bones break the ties that bind them like constellations, there will be a fabulous noise, a noise catastrophic for sensitive musical ears, more violent than that of distant things breaking free, escaping at a gallop. Such is the anxiety of the escaped prisoner, who makes the roads howl and startles gutless time, time that mimics the gestures of the universe.

Ladies and gentlemen: The viper from the shipwrecks bites its own tail and grows infinitely larger.

Inside its coils we are sucked down into the abyss of impending decay, pus oozing from our eyes like spume deposited on the shore. Meanwhile the landscapes within us sense the flight of trees; our ears, before coming off and falling like leaves, still manage to hear the whirlwind of sinking wheat fields. There is no hope of rest. In vain, the skeleton behind the

cantar. Las puertas internas del planeta se cubren los oídos con violencia, como el enfermero que oye los alaridos de la terrible aventura en la última frontera. Nada se gana con pensar que acaso detrás de la muralla abstracta se extiende la zona voluptuosa del asombro.

No, no encontraréis al anciano sentado sobre las rocas de la nevazón eterna, sonriendo sin dureza y rodeado de héroes meditativos como palmeras.

Dos palabras aún, amigos míos, antes de terminar: Vanas son nuestras luchas y nuestras discusiones, vana la fosforescencia de nuestras espadas y de nuestras palabras. Sólo el ataúd tiene razón. La victoria es del cementerio. El triunfo sólo florece en el sembrado misterioso.

Así fue el discurso que habéis llamado macabro sin razón alguna, el bello discurso del presentador de la nada.

Pasad. Seguid vuestro camino como yo sigo ahora.

Soy demasiado lento para morir.

Sin embargo, Isolda, prepara tus lágrimas. Lejana, enternecida como un piano de remordimientos, prepara tus mejores lágrimas.

Soy lento para morir. La estatua se pasea sobre el mar y el viento cierra mis párpados en señal de gloria penetrante.

Una montaña ocupa la mitad de mi pecho.

Yo llevo un corazón demasiado grande para vosotros. Vosotros habéis medido vuestras montañas, vosotros sabéis que el Gaurizankar tiene 8.800 metros de altura, pero vosotros no sabéis ni sabréis jamás la altura de mi corazón. Sin embargo, mañana en el fondo de la tierra escucharé vuestros pasos.

¿Quién turbará el silencio? Acallad ese ruido insolente.

Son mis antepasados que bailan sobre mi tumba. Son mis abuelos que tocan a rebato para despertarme.

Es el jefe de la tribu que se encuentra solo y que llora.

Acallad vuestros gritos inútiles.

Henos al fin dormidos en el carne de la tierra.

Desde entonces vive el cataclismo en las ciudades. Caen las murallas y los techos dejando ver pueblos enteros desnudos en diversas actitudes, las más de las veces implorando misericordia.

Asoman brazos y piernas entre escombros.

Hubo también entonces un derrumbe en el cielo. Cuántos pájaros murieron aplastados.

window strikes the hieratic pose of one about to sing. The planet's inner doors violently cover their ears, like a nurse hearing the clamour from the terrible adventure at the final frontier. Nothing is gained by thinking that the voluptuous realm of wonder stretches beyond the abstract wall.

No, you will not find the old man sitting on the rocks of eternal snowfall, smiling softly, surrounded by meditative heroes like palm trees.

A couple of words more, my friends, before I finish: our struggles and arguments are in vain, our phosphorescing swords and our words are in vain. Only the coffin is correct. Victory belongs to the cemetery. Only in that mysterious sown field does triumph flourish.

Such was the speech that, for no reason, you have called grim, the beautiful speech of the presenter of the void.

Go on. Follow your path, as I follow mine.

I am too slow in dying.

Nevertheless, Isolde, prepare your tears. Distant, softened like a piano of remorse, prepare your finest tears.

I am slow to die. The statue wanders over the sea and the wind closes my eyelids in a sign of piercing glory.

A mountain takes up half my chest.

I have too big a heart for you. You have measured your mountains, you know that Gaurishankar is 8,800 metres high, but you do not know, nor will you ever know, the elevation of my heart. Yet tomorrow, from deep within the earth, I will hear your footsteps.

Who will disturb the peace? Silence this insolent noise.

Those are my forebears dancing on my grave. My ancestors sounding the alarm to wake me.

It is the leader of the tribe, standing alone and weeping.

Hush your useless cries.

Here we are at last, asleep in the earth's flesh.

Since then the cataclysm abides in the cities. Walls and roofs have collapsed, revealing entire peoples naked in various poses, more often than not begging for mercy.

Arms and legs protrude from the rubble.

Then too the sky caved in. How many birds perished, crushed.

Días después las gentes se paseaban mirando las ruinas. No quedó una sonrisa en pie. Pasaban los fantasmas con los ojos cubiertos aullando, y un hombre enloquecido saltaba de cabeza con el puñal en la mano buscando a un dios culpable.

Sudad, esclavos, levantad las ciudades futuras. Yo entretanto miro la carrera de las selvas. Yo contemplo el pirata del ocaso y su lento suplicio.

Medid la tierra para saber cuántos milagros caben. Adornad los volcanes, embanderad los ríos, horadad las montañas. Vosotros me diréis mañana cuántos fantasmas se pueden enterrar aún con todos sus sueños.

Despierta, Isolda, antes que venga la revuelta final y tu lecho quede acribillado por las balas porque nadie cree en tu verdad.

Será preciso, te digo, que tu gracia se levante entre cadáveres, tu gracia cogida en las ruedas del motín, mientras el fuego lo destruye todo y empieza a lamer el horizonte y a trepar por el cielo.

Se doblan las torres bajo la lluvia ilimitada. Vuelan techos ardiendo.

Todo ha de pasar.

De borde a borde el mundo está en silencio. Pero hay algo que aún nos busca en todas partes.

Arad la tierra para sembrar prodigios. Lanzad escalas por todos los abismos.

Decidme, ¿qué utilidad presenta la esperanza? Se alejan los veleros en su Gólgota interminable, por miedo a la borrasca. Atrás se queda todo.

La canoa que debe perecer va subiendo la última ola.

El cielo es lento para morir.

¿Oyes clavar el ataúd del cielo?

For days afterwards people wandered through the ruins. Not even a smile was left standing. Ghosts passed by with covered eyes, howling, and a crazed man leaped headlong, dagger in hand, looking for a guilty god.

Sweat, slaves, raise up the cities of the future. Meanwhile I watch the progress of the forests. I behold the pirate of sunset and his slow torment.

Measure the earth to learn how many miracles it can hold. Adorn the volcanoes, deck rivers out with flags, tunnel through mountains. You will tell me tomorrow how many ghosts might yet be buried with all their dreams.

Awake, Isolde, before the final uprising comes, and your bed is riddled with bullets because no-one believed in your truth.

It will be necessary, I tell you, for your grace to rise amongst the corpses, your grace caught in the wheels of the riot, while fire consumes it all and begins to lick at the horizon, to climb into the sky.

Towers buckle under the incessant rain. Burning roofs fly through the air.

All things must pass.

From end to end the world is in silence. But there is something that still searches for us everywhere.

Plough the earth and sow wonders. Throw ladders across all chasms.

Tell me, what use is hope? Sailing ships move away on their endless Golgotha, for fear of storms. Everything is left behind.

The canoe that ought to perish is already cresting the final wave.

The sky is slow to die.

Do you hear the sky's coffin being nailed shut?

SKYQUAKE

TREMBLEMENT DE CIEL

First of all it should be known how often we have to abandon our bride and flee from sex to sex right to the ends of the earth.

There where the void draws its violin bow across the horizon and a man turns into a bird and an angel into a precious stone.

The Eternal Father manufactures darkness in his laboratory, striving to turn blind men deaf. He keeps one eye in his hand and knows not on whom to pin it. And in a jar he keeps an ear making love to another eye.

We are far away, at the end of all things where a man, hanging by his feet from a star, swings head-down in space. The wind that bends the trees gently ruffles his hair.

Flying streams land in new forests where birds curse the appearance of so many useless flowers.

How right they are to insult the fluttering of these dark things.

If only it were enough to slit the throat of the captain of flowers and make his heart bleed with superfluous feelings, a heart full of secrets and pieces of the universe.

The mouth of a beloved man upon a drum.

The breasts of the unforgettable young girl nailed to the same tree where nightingales can peck at them.

And the hero's statue at the Pole.

It must all be destroyed, all of it, with bullet and blade.

Idols fight it out under water.

Isolde, Isolde, how many kilometres separate us, how many sexes between you and me.

You well know that God plucks out the eyes of flowers, for he is obsessed with blindness.

And he turns the spirit into a bundle of feathers and turns brides seated on roses into pianola snakes, into snakes that are sister to the flute, the same flute that is kissed on snowy nights and that calls to them from afar.

But you do not know why the blackbird shreds the tree with its bloody talons.

And there lies the mystery.

Forty days and forty nights climbing from branch to branch as in the days of the Flood. Forty days and forty nights of mystery among the rocks and mountains.

I might fall from destiny to destiny, but I will always retain the memory of the sky.

D'abord il faut savoir combien de fois nous devons abandonner notre fiancée et fuir de sexe en sexe jusqu'à la fin de la terre.

Là, où le vide passe son archet sur l'horizon et l'homme se transforme en oiseau et l'ange en pierre précieuse.

Le Père Éternel fabrique des ténèbres dans son laboratoire, il travaille pour rendre sourds les aveugles. Il a un œil dans la main et ne sait pas sur qui le visser. Dans un bocal il a une oreille faisant l'amour avec un autre œil.

Nous sommes loin, au bout des bouts, où un homme pendu par les pieds d'une étoile se balance dans l'espace, la tête en bas. Le vent qui penche les arbres agite doucement ses cheveux.

Les ruisseaux volants se posent sur les forêts nouvelles où les oiseaux maudissent le réveil de tant de fleurs inutiles.

Ils ont bien raison d'insulter les palpitations de ces choses obscures.

S'il s'agissait seulement d'égorger le capitaine des fleurs et faire saigner son cœur au sentiment superflu, le cœur plein de secrets et de morceaux d'univers.

La bouche d'un homme aimé sur un tambour.

Les seins de la jeune fille inoubliable cloués au même arbre où les rossignols peuvent les becqueter.

Et la statue du héros au pôle.

Il faut tout détruire, tout, au fusil et au couteau.

Les idoles se battent sous l'eau.

Iseult, Iseult, combien de kilomètres nous séparent, combien de sexes entre toi et moi.

Tu sais bien que Dieu arrache les yeux aux fleurs, car sa manie est la cécité.

Il transforme l'esprit en un paquet de plumes et transforme les fiancées assises sur des roses en serpents de pianola, en serpents sœurs de la flûte, de la même flûte qui s'embrasse dans les nuits de neige, et qui les appelle de loin.

Mais tu ne sais pas pour quelle raison le merle déchire l'arbre entre ses doigts saignants.

Et voilà le mystère.

Quarante jours et quarante nuits, grimpant de branche en branche comme pendant le déluge. Quarante jours et quarante nuits de mystère parmi les rochers et les montagnes.

Je peux tomber de destin en destin mais je garderai toujours le souvenir du ciel.

Have you experienced visions from on high? Have you seen the heart of the light? At times I become a vast forest and march across worlds like an army.

Look at the river mouth.

On some evenings the sea can barely even serve as my theatre.

The street of dreams has no trees, no woman crucified in a flower, no boat sailing the pages of the sea.

The street of dreams has an enormous navel from which a bottle neck protrudes. Inside the bottle there is a dead bishop. The bishop changes colour whenever the bottle moves.

There are four candles that light up and go out one after another. Sometimes a flash of lightning reveals in the sky a dismembered woman who has been falling for one hundred and forty years.

The sky conceals its mystery.

On every stairway one suspects a hidden killer. Faint-hearted singers die at the very thought of it.

So it is that sickly butterflies will return to the larval state they should never have left. The ear will fall back into childhood and will fill with echoes of the sea and with that seaweed which floats in the eyes of some birds.

Only Isolde knows the mystery. But she runs her trembling fingers along the rainbow, seeking a special sound.

And if a blackbird pecks at her eye, she lets it drink all the water it wants, with the same smile that attracts herds of buffalo.

On which heart, swollen with bitterness, could you float on all the oceans, on any sea?

Surely you must know that it is dangerous to cling to a heart as if it were a buoy, because of the sea caves that attract them, and the octopi, like knots of snakes or elephant trunks, block the exit forever.

Realise what a mountain is like, with its arms raised, begging forgiveness, and bear in mind that it is less dangerous than the seas and more amenable to friendship.

However it is your destiny to love danger, the danger that lies within you and without you, to kiss the lips of the abyss, relying on shadowy forces for the ultimate success of all your ventures and your dreams, drenched in dew at daybreak.

If not, give thanks and withdraw into the depths of mankind's memory.

Connais-tu les visions de la hauteur? As-tu vu le cœur de la lumière. Parfois je deviens une forêt immense et je parcours les mondes comme une armée.

Regarde l'entrée des rivières.

La mer peut à peine être mon théâtre certains soirs.

La rue des rêves n'a pas d'arbres, ni une femme crucifiée dans une fleur ni un bateau passant les pages de la mer.

La rue des rêves a un nombril immense, d'où surgit le goulot d'une bouteille. À l'intérieur de la bouteille il y a un évêque mort. L'évêque change de couleur chaque fois que la bouteille bouge.

Il y a quatre bougies qui s'allument et s'éteignent l'une après l'autre.

Parfois un éclair nous fait voir dans le ciel une femme déchiquetée qui tombe depuis cent quarante ans.

Le ciel cache son mystère.

Dans tous les escaliers on soupçonne un assassin caché. Les chanteurs cardiaques meurent à cette seule pensée.

Ainsi les papillons maladifs reviendront à leur état de ver d'où ils n'auraient jamais dû sortir. L'ouie retombera en enfance et se remplira d'échos marins et de ces algues qui flottent dans les yeux de certains oiseaux.

Seulement Iseult connaît le mystère. Mais elle parcourt l'arc-en-ciel avec ses doigts tremblants à la recherche d'un son spécial.

Et si un merle becquète son œil elle le laisse boire tout l'eau qu'il veut avec ce même sourire qui attire les troupeaux de buffles.

Sur quel cœur gonflé d'amertume pourrais-tu flotter dans tous les océans, dans n'importe quelle mer?

Parce que tu dois savoir que s'agripper à un cœur comme à une bouée est dangereux à cause des grottes marines qui les attirent et dont les poulpes qui sont des nœuds de serpents ou des trompes d'éléphants leur ferment la sortie pour toujours.

Rends-toi compte de ce qu'est une montagne les bras levés, demandant pardon, et pense qu'elle est moins dangereuse que les mers, et plus accessible à l'amitié.

Cependant ton destin est d'aimer le danger, le danger qui est en toi et en dehors de toi, de baiser les lèvres de l'abîme, en comptant sur des aides ténébreuses pour le succès final de toutes tes entreprises et de tes rêves couverts de rosée au point du jour.

Si non, remercie et retire-toi jusqu'au fond de la mémoire des hommes.

—Isolde, Isolde, in the Ice Age bears were flowers. When the thaw came they freed themselves and ran off in all directions.

Think of the resurrection and take a moment to reflect.

You alone know the miracle. You have seen the miracle performed in the presence of a hundred awestruck harps and all the cannons aimed at the horizon.

There was then a procession of sailors before a king in a far-off land. The waves impatiently awaited their return, while the sea applauded.

The thermometer dropped slowly because the blackbird had stopped singing and was thinking of leaping from a trapeze at the centre of the world.

Now I fear only one thing, that you might emerge from a lamp or a vase and speak to me in eloquent terms the way magnolias speak in the evening. The room would be filled with dying dragonflies and I would have to sit down so as not to faint.

Death would be thought itself. Reflected everywhere where eyes might settle.

Above the castle the general's skeleton will signal like a semaphore. We will count the skulls dragged across the field by an endless rope tied to the tail of a sleepwalking horse that no-one claims as their own.

Black men will applaud oer the bellies of slave women as intoxicated as they are unaware that the wind is a ghost and that the trees are floating above a cemetery far away.

Who has counted all their dead?

And if all the windows were opened and all the lamps began to sing and the cemetery caught fire?

For every bird in the sky there will be a hunter on the ground.

Bugles will sound and flags will turn into sparklers. Faith is dead; dead too are the birds of prey that gnawed at your heart.

Migrating statues fly by. On the vast plain the torment of idols can be heard amidst the singing trees.

Flowers flee in terror.

The doors of an unknown music open and out come the years of the sorcerer who remains seated in his agony, hands on his chest.

How many things have died inside us. How many dead do we carry within us. Why do we cling to our dead? Why do we persist in reviving our dead? They prevent us from seeing ideas being born. We fear the new

—Iseult, Iseult, à l'époque glaciaire les ours étaient des fleurs. Lorsqu' arriva le dégel ils se libérèrent d'eux-mêmes et s'échappèrent en courant dans toutes les directions.

Pense à la résurrection et recueille-toi un moment.

Toi seule tu connais le miracle. Tu as vu le miracle se réaliser devant cent harpes émerveillées et tous les canons pointant vers l'horizon.

Il y avait alors un défilé de matelots devant un roi dans un pays lointain. Les vagues attendaient impatientes le retour des siens. Pendant ce temps la mer applaudissait.

Le thermomètre descendait, lentement, parce que le merle avait cessé de chanter et il pensait s'élancer d'un trapèze au milieu du monde.

Maintenant je ne crains qu'une chose, que tu sortes d'une lampe ou d'un fleurier et que tu me parles en termes éloquents comme les magnolias parlent le soir. La chambre se remplirait de libellules agonisantes et je devrais m'asseoir pour ne pas tomber sans connaissance.

La mort serait la pensée même. Reflétée partout où se posent les yeux.

Sur le château le squelette du général fera des signaux comme un sémaphore. Nous compterons les têtes de morts traînées à travers le champ par une corde interminable attachée à la queue d'un cheval somnambule que personne ne reconnaît comme sien.

Les noirs applaudiront sur les ventres des esclaves aussi ivres qu'eux sans se rendre compte que le vent est un fantôme et que les arbres loin là-bas flottent sur un cimetière.

Qui a compté tous ses morts?

Et si on ouvrait toutes les fenêtres, et si toutes les lampes se mettaient à chanter et si le cimetière prenait feu?

Pour chaque oiseau dans le ciel il y aura un chasseur sur la terre.

Les clairons sonneront et les drapeaux deviendront des feux de Bengale. Morte la foi, morts les oiseaux de proie qui te rongeaient le cœur.

Les statues migratrices passent en volant. Dans la plaine immense on entend le supplice des idoles au milieu des chants des arbres.

Les fleurs fuient épouvantées.

Les portes d'une musique inconnue s'ouvrent, les années du mage sortent et il reste assis agonisant, les mains sur la poitrine.

Combien de choses sont mortes en nous. Combien de morts nous portons en nous. À quoi bon nous agripper à nos morts? Pourquoi nous obstinons-nous à ressusciter nos morts? Ils nous empêchent de voir l'idée qui naît. Nous avons peur de la nouvelle lumière qui se présente, à laquelle

light that comes along, one we are not yet accustomed to, as we are to our motionless dead, who lack dangerous surprises. The dead have to be left behind for the sake of the living.

—Isolde, bury all your dead.

Think, remember, forget. May your memory forget your memories, may your forgetfulness remember what is forgotten. Take care not to die before your death.

How does one grant a little greatness to this present-day creature that only bends its weary knees at this late hour when the moon comes flying in and stands before you.

And yet we live in hope of some chance occurrence, the appearance of an astral sign in this allegorical beyond, where not even the sound of our bells can penetrate.

Waiting, in this way, for the great chance.

Let the North Pole come off like a hat raised in greeting.

Let the continent we have been waiting for these many years emerge, seated here behind the bars of the horizon.

Let the killer run past, firing wild shots at his pursuers.

Let it be known why it was a girl that was born and not the boy promised in dreams and foretold so many times.

Let the corpse appear yawning and stretching beneath the earth.

Let the glorious ghost be seen passing along the avenues of the sky.

Let all rivers be halted suddenly at one single command.

Let the sky change location.

Let the seas pile up into a great pyramid higher than all the towers dreamed of by ambition.

Let a desperate wind blow and extinguish the stars.

Let a luminous finger write a word in the night sky.

Let the house across the street collapse.

For this do we live, believe me, for this do we live and for nothing else. For this we have a voice and for this our voice has a net.

And for this we have that anxious racing in our veins and that wounded animal galloping in our chest.

nous ne sommes pas encore habitués comme à nos morts immobiles et sans surprise dangereuse. Il faut abandonner ce qui est mort pour ce qui est vivant.

—Iseult, enterre tous tes morts.

Pense, souviens-toi, oublie. Que ton souvenir oublie ses souvenirs, que ton oubli se souvienne de ses oublis. Prends garde de ne pas mourir avant ta mort.

Comment donner un peu de grandeur à cette bête actuelle qui seulement plie ses genoux de fatigue à ces hautes heures quand la lune arrive en volant et se place en face.

Et pourtant nous vivons en attendant un hasard, la formation d'un signe sidéral, dans cet allégorique au-delà, où n'arrive même pas le son de nos cloches.

Ainsi, attendant le grand hasard.

Que le pôle nord se détache comme le chapeau qui salue.

Que surgisse le continent que nous attendons depuis tant d'années, assis derrière les grilles de l'horizon.

Que l'assassin passe en courant et tirant sans contrôle sur ses poursuivants.

Que l'on sache pourquoi est née cette fille et non le garçon promis par les rêves et annoncé tant de fois.

Que l'on voie le cadavre qui bâille et s'étire sous la terre.

Que l'on voie passer le fantôme glorieux dans les allées du ciel.

Que tout d'un coup s'arrêtent toutes les rivières à une voix de commandement.

Que le ciel change de place.

Que les mers s'amoncellent en une grande pyramide plus haute que toutes les tours rêvées par l'ambition.

Que souffle un vent désespéré, qui éteigne les étoiles.

Qu'un doigt lumineux écrive un mot dans le ciel de la nuit.

Que s'écroule la maison d'en face.

Pour cela nous vivons, tu peux me croire, c'est pour cela que nous vivons et non pour autre chose. Pour cela nous avons une voix et pour cela nous avons un filet dans la voix.

Pour cela nous avons ce courir angoissé dans les veines et ce galop d'animal blessé dans la poitrine.

It is for this that the flesh of words reddens in martyrdom, and thought grows, watered by underground rivers. That is why we have inherited the howl of our most tragic of our ancestors.

Cut off the head of the monster roaring at dream's door. And then let no one forbid anything.

Someone speaks and a water-lily appears at the voice's pinnacle before the opium of the future gaze can glitter.

—Peace on earth to the night sailor.

Silent explorers raise their heads and the adventure is stripped of its golden costume.

This is the meaning of sunset.

Perhaps the sunset will want to listen to us and then you will understand the signs of the night. You will understand the inventions of silence. The gaze of dreams. The threshold of the abyss. The journey through the mountains.

The crossing of the night.

Isolde, Isolde, I am following my destiny.

Where did you hide the oasis you promised me so many times?

The light grew weary of moving.

Tell me, where does this stairway lead, the one that leaves your eyes and then vanishes into the air?

Do you know it is my destiny to walk? Do you recognise the explorer's vanity and the ghost of adventure?

It is a matter of flesh and blood being confronted by a special magnet. It is an irrevocable fate for a meteor out of legend.

It is not a matter of fleshly love, it is a matter of life, a matter of a travelling spirit, of a nomadic bird.

All these women are trees, or resting stones along the path, perhaps none of them necessary.

Bottles of water or barrels of inebriation, mostly without their own light. Like cathedrals they adhere to a musical principle. Each chord has its counterpart and everything depends on knowing how to strike the echo point, which has to respond. It is simple to weave sounds together and construct a genuine roof or magnificent domes for rainy days.

If destiny so permits, we can stop for a while and count the fingers of whoever holds her arms out to us.

Pour cela rougit la chair martyrisée des mots et pousse la pensée arrosée par les rivières souterraines. Pour cela le hurlement du sursaut hérité de l'aïeul le plus tragique.

Coupez la tête au monstre qui rugit à la porte du rêve. Et après que personne n'interdise rien.

Quelqu'un parle et il pousse un nénuphar au sommet de sa voix avant que brille l'opium du regard futur.

—Paix sur la terre au matelot de la nuit.

Les explorateurs silencieux lèvent la tête et l'aventure se dépouille de ses vêtements d'or.

Voici le sens du couchant.

Peut-être le couchant voudra nous écouter et alors vous comprendrez les signes de la nuit. Vous comprendrez les inventions du silence. Le regard du rêve. Le seuil de l'abîme. Le voyage des montagnes.

La traversée de la nuit.

Iseult, Iseult, je suis mon destin.

Où as-tu caché l'oasis que tu m'avais promise tant de fois?

La lumière s'est fatiguée de marcher.

Où conduit, dis-moi, cet escalier qui sort de tes yeux et se perd dans l'air?

Sais-tu que mon destin est de marcher? Connais-tu la vanité de l'explorateur et le fantôme de l'aventure?

C'est une question de sang et d'os devant un aimant spécial. C'est un destin irrévocable de météore fabuleux.

Ce n'est pas une question d'amour en chair c'est une question de vie, une question d'esprit voyageur, d'oiseau nomade.

Toutes ces femmes sont des arbres, ou des pierres de repos dans le chemin, peut-être pas nécessaires.

Des bouteilles d'eau ou des tonneaux d'ivresse, généralement sans lumière propre. Elles obéissent comme les cathédrales à un principe musical. Chaque accord a son correspondant et tout consiste à savoir toucher le point de l'écho qui doit répondre. Il est facile de faire des tissus de sons et de construire une véritable toiture ou de magnifiques coupoles pour les jours de pluie.

Si le destin le permet nous pouvons nous garer pour un temps et compter les doigts de celle qui nous tend les bras.

After that the ghost will force us to proceed. We will leap over the heaving breasts that form domes because, lying on her back, she is like a temple. Or rather, it is a case of temples imitating them, with their breast-like towers, their central dome like a head and their doorway that seeks to imitate the vulva where one enters looking for the life that pulses in the womb, and through which that same life must issue forth.

But we do not have to accept such imitations, nor can we believe in such a life. In this life which emerges, blindfolded, and stumbles against all the trees in the countryside. We will only believe in flowers that are cradles for giants, although we know that inside each bud there sleeps a dwarf.

And in the background, the mountains of living rock smile sweetly.

The mountains smile because a blind man has sat down on them to hear the drumming of the volcano. But what happens on the plains is even more important, for the trees in the forest have turned into snakes, writhing rhythmically to the sound of a special flute.

I forgot to tell you there is also a lake, and that this lake moves further away with every puff of wind. Sometimes it is lost from view, sometimes it is gone for long years and returns a different colour. Sometimes it is hungry and curses men who fail to be shipwrecked at the appointed time. At other times it walks on all fours and gnaws for hours and hours on the scraps of so many tragedies washed up on its shores, or on the reflections of certain secret times.

If the bird in the eye falls into the waters, a geyser erupts in the mountains. A geyser as beautiful as a tree, with a woman balancing at its tip.

The lake too can balance on top of the tree. Everything depends on my will and on the drum beating time.

All those spies hiding behind trees are not waiting for the miracle, as they would have us believe, but for the naked blind woman who emerges in the evening to walk with her lost statue and who might collide with them.

You are wasting your time.

Look, look, there is a fire on the moon.

Dressed in white, Isolde arrived like a cloud.

Then the moon began to fall, enveloped in flames. On the beaches there danced a reflection of fire.

Spectres emerged one by one from every rising wave. You who are hidden there, the hour has come to tremble before the voracity of death.

Après, le fantôme nous obligera à suivre la marche. Nous sauterons pardessus les seins palpitants qui sont des coupoles parce qu'elle, étendue sur le dos, imite un temple. Mieux dit, ce sont les temples qui les imitent, elles, avec leurs tours comme des seins, leur coupole centrale comme une tête leur porte qui voudrait imiter le sexe, par où on entre chercher la vie qui palpite dans le ventre et par où doit sortir après la même vie.

Mais nous ne devons pas accepter une semblable imitation et nous ne pouvons pas croire à une telle vie. À cette vie qui sort avec les yeux bandés et va se heurtant à tous les arbres du paysage. Seulement nous croirons aux fleurs qui sont berceaux de géants, bien que nous sachions qu'en dedans de chaque bouton dort un nain moqueur.

Et au fond les montagnes de roche vivante sourient doucement.

Les montagnes sourient parce qu'un aveugle s'est assis sur elles pour entendre rouler le tambour du volcan. Mais ce qui se passe clans les plaines est encore beaucoup plus important, car les arbres du bois sont devenus serpents et se débattent rythmiquement à cause d'une flûte spéciale.

J'oubliais de vous dire qu'il y a aussi un lac et que ce lac s'éloigne suivant le souffle du vent. Parfois on arrive jusqu'à le perdre de vue, parfois il passe de longues années absent et revient d'une autre couleur. Parfois il a faim et il maudit les hommes qui ne font pas naufrage à l'heure dû. D'autres fois il marche à quatre pattes et ronge pendant des heures et des heures, les épaves de tant de tragédies accumulées sur ses rives ou les reflets de certains temps secrets.

Si l'oiseau de l'œil tombe dans ses eaux il saute un geyser dans la montagne. Un geyser beau comme un arbre avec une femme en équilibre au bout.

Aussi le lac pourrait s'équilibrer sur la pointe de l'arbre. Tout dépend de ma volonté et du tambour qui roule à temps.

Tous ces espions cachés derrière les arbres n'attendent pas le miracle comme ils voudraient le faire croire, mais la femme nue et aveugle qui sort les soirs promener sa statue perdue et qui pourrait se heurter à eux.

Tu gaspilles ton temps.

Regardez, regardez, il y a un incendie dans la lune.

Vêtue de blanc Iseult venait comme un nuage.

Alors la lune commença à tomber entourée de flammes. Dans les plages dansait un reflet de feu.

Les spectres sortent un à un de chaque vague qui se lève. Vous qui êtes là cachés, l'heure de trembler devant la voracité de la mort est arrivée.

The setting sun forms a halo over the head of the last shipwrecked sailor who floats adrift, no longer able to hear any singing from the shore.

Wolves roam with glowing eyes amidst the foliage of night, bound tightly together and weeping for no real reason.

That man there, taller than the others, opens his mouth in the middle of the garden and begins swallowing fireflies for hour after hour.

The trees are twisted by a strange pain.

And numerous meteors falling from the sky create spirals in our atmosphere as if they were stones thrown into water.

Thick smoke billows everywhere. Now the only things that glow are the eyes of wolves and the man full of fireflies. All the rest is gloom.

The mountain opens its doors and the blind man enters with outstretched arms.

There is a great tree writhing in the fire of dusk.

Up above, God rocks a new-born planet.

Halos fall upon the earth. One after another hundreds of halos fall upon the earth, some of them onto heads… And nothing more?

An island of palm trees surges up from the sea for the newly-weds walking arm in arm.

One day perhaps one of them will find the head they had lost, motionless in the very place where it had been lost.

When? Where? Which one of them?

Here there is torment, Isolde, beyond the mountain. There is torment there.

The migrating forests will not reach this far.

There is a solitary sandal at the centre of the earth.

The passage of evenings can be heard at the bottom of the sea, at the moment when everything glows with intoxication.

There is a hat higher up, at head height.

There is a staff driven into the soil, at hand height.

And there is nothing more. Because none of you can see the ghost smiling at the dog at this moment.

No one knows why the curtains behind the bed moved.

Nor why Isolde's cheeks blushed like two curtains being drawn.

And why her legs trembled like two curtains being opened.

* * *

Le soleil couchant fait une auréole sur la tête du dernier naufragé qui flotte à la dérive, sans entendre les chants du rivage.

Les loups se promènent les yeux brillants parmi les branches de la nuit, enlacés étroitement et pleurants sans cause précise.

Cet homme-là plus grand que les autres ouvre la bouche au milieu du jardin et commence à avaler des lucioles pendant de longues heures.

Les arbres sont tordus à cause d'une douleur étrange.

Et une quantité de météores qui tombent du ciel forment des spirales dans notre atmosphère comme si c'étaient des pierres dans l'eau.

Une fumée épaisse sort de partout. Maintenant seuls brillent les yeux des loups et l'homme plein de lucioles. Tout le reste est pénombre.

La montagne ouvre ses portes et l'aveugle rentre les bras tendus.

Il y a un arbre gros qui se tord dans le feu du crépuscule.

En haut, Dieu berce un astre nouveau-né.

Il tombe des auréoles sur la terre. L'une après l'autre elles tombent, des centaines d'auréoles sur la terre, quelques-unes sur certaines têtes… Et rien de plus?

Une île de palmiers jaillit de la mer pour les fiancés qui se promènent embrassés.

Un jour peut-être l'un d'eux retrouvera la tête qu'il avait perdue, immobile, à la même place où il la perdit.

Quand? où? lequel d'entre eux?

Voici le supplice, Iseult, derrière la montagne. Voilà le supplice.

Les forêts migratrices n'arriveront pas si loin.

Il y a une sandale seule au milieu de la terre.

La marche des soirs qui passent s'entend au fond de la mer, à ce moment où tout devient brillant d'ivresse.

Il y a un chapeau plus haut, à la hauteur d'une tête.

Il y a une canne clouée dans le sol à la hauteur d'une main.

Et il n'y a rien de plus. Parce que personne parmi vous ne peut voir le fantôme qui sourit au chien en cet instant.

Personne ne sait pourquoi les rideaux derrière le lit remuèrent.

Ni pourquoi rougirent les joues d'Iseult comme deux rideaux qui s'écartent.

Et pourquoi tremblèrent ses jambes comme deux rideaux qui s'ouvrent.

* * *

Upon waking I could weep to see you smile.

I could beg a greeting from the spectre that is headed solemnly for the Stone Age.

You know this well, for you I will pass like a reflection from forest to forest. What more do you want?

Two bodies entwined tame eternity.

And they have to get down on their knees.

Then the castle turns into a flower, the ear into a river full of boats and all kinds of fish.

The piano turns into a mountain, the sea into a little artichoke that spins like a windmill.

The nerves turn into a tree full of tremors and its tremors multiply repeatedly through the night until infinity.

The brain rolls down the body and vanishes who knows where. At the same moment the forests flee in disorder.

Here the ordeal of the bones begins with sacks of clouds on their backs, coming down from the peak of the silent womb, sad as a witch's bird, sad as the flower threatened by the night.

Prepared by solitude, everything is possible. Besides, hanging from each chandelier, a woman swings through the air we breathe. Music emerges from each picture nailed to the wall, since we know that every landscape is a musical instrument. And behind each door there is an impatient skeleton waiting.

Completely abandoned, the night weeps in its retreat. The night that sounded your heart. The night—do you remember?—when curtains took on the shape of ears and the shape of eyelids with silent lashes. Then I leaned over you as if over a dissecting table, sank my lips into you and watched you; your belly resembling a fresh wound and your eyes like the end of the world.

Dragged down by solitude, Isolde, we sank into the night that awaited us at the foot of the house.

* * *

We walked a great deal. Searchlights scanned desperately through the night, from one side to the other, crossed paths at infinity, greeted one another and said farewell forever. Suddenly a hand appeared in the midst of the sky,

Je serai capable de pleurer à mon réveil pour te voir sourire.

Je serai capable de mendier le salut du spectre qui marche solennel vers l'âge de pierre.

Tu le sais bien, pour toi je passerai comme un reflet de forêt en forêt. Que veux-tu de plus?

Deux corps enlacés domptent l'éternité.

Et il faut se mettre à genoux.

Alors le château devient une fleur, l'œil devient une rivière pleine de barques et de toutes espèces de poissons.

Le piano devient une montagne, la mer un petit artichaut qui tourne comme un moulin.

Les nerfs deviennent un arbre plein de tremblements et leurs tremblements se propagent dans la nuit d'espace en espace jusqu'à l'infini.

Le cerveau dévale le long du corps, et s'en va on ne sait où. Au même instant les forêts fuient en débandade.

Ici commence le supplice des os avec leur sac de nuages au dos descendant du sommet de la matrice silencieuse, triste comme l'oiseau d'une sorcière, comme la fleur menacée par la nuit.

Préparé par la solitude tout est possible. D'ailleurs, pendue de chaque lustre une femme se berce dans l'air que nous respirons. Il sort une musique de chaque tableau cloué au mur puisque nous savons que tout paysage est un instrument musical. Et derrière chaque porte il y a un squelette impatient qui attend.

La nuit pleure dans sa retraite, complètement abandonnée. La nuit qui t'auscultait le cœur. La nuit te souviens-tu quand les rideaux prenaient forme d'oreilles et forme de paupières avec des cils de silence. Alors je m'inclinais sur toi comme sur un table de dissection, je plongeais en toi mes lèvres et je te regardais; ton ventre semblable à une blessure vivante et tes yeux comme la fin du monde.

Traînés par la solitude, Iseult, nous avons sombré dans la nuit qui nous attendait au pied de la maison.

* * *

Nous avons beaucoup marché. Les réflecteurs cherchaient désespérés dans la nuit, ils couraient d'un côté à l'autre, se croisaient dans l'infini, se saluaient et se disaient adieu pour toujours. Soudain une main sortit du milieu du

a hand like that of a castaway, and crushed between its fingers the head of a bird that fell slowly to the ground, without a single complaint from its lips.

We were by the sea. A wave came rushing in, took the dead bird and carried it away.

The mountain by the shore shivered slightly, and then from its cetacean back spouted a jet of fresh, crystalline water while a wave rolled over the lighthouse, which appeared as if inside a distant display-case.

Thus returned the hour of serenity, led by the hand of a comet that no-one knew what to name and which the children called, no-one ever knew why, Eloise's Hair.

Sometimes, at night, the eye can still be seen floating on the sea like a desolate almond.

Sometimes the trawler can still be seen passing through the air with its nets extended.

Sometimes the drowned man can still be seen rocked between two waters, his body glowing.

Sometimes the sailing boat can still be seen like a cross on its never-ending Golgotha.

Sometimes pirates can still be seen clinging to the keel and their captain hanging from the mainmast on the open sea.

In a flash of lightning, the pale helmsman can still be seen, his beard to the wind.

In a flash of lightning, the naked beauty can still be seen, her breasts swollen.

In a flash of lightning, the kidnapper's horse can still be seen vanishing in the distance.

Sometimes, on moonlit nights, the floating hand can still be seen.

But mermaids, fishing with their hair meshed into nets, have not been seen again, and we waited in vain.

We have greeted all the waves, watched attentively, waved our hats and handkerchiefs, gambled their breasts at dice on board thousands of ships. All in vain. Dawn's accomplices heard the flowers on their journey, heard the progress of the polar light and once again the hero's advance towards the Stone Age.

But no-one will see the ordeal of the mermaids.

In vain do you raise your fingers, pointing to every fold in the sea and every tremor in the clouds.

ciel une main comme d'un naufragé et écrasa entre ses doigts la tête d'un oiseau qui tomba, sans un reproche de ses lèvres, lentement sur la terre.

Nous étions au bord de la mer. Une vague arriva en courant, prit l'oiseau mort et l'emporta.

La montagne de la rive frissonna légèrement, puis de son dos de cétacé jaillit un jet d'eau frais et cristallin tandis qu'une vague passait par-dessus le phare qui parut en dedans d'une vitrine lointaine.

Ainsi revînt l'heure de la sérénité conduite à la main par une comète que personne ne sut baptiser et que les enfants appelèrent, jamais on ne sut pourquoi, chevelure d'Héloïse.

Encore, parfois, on peut voir pendant les nuits, l'œil qui flotte sur la mer comme une amande désolée.

Encore, parfois, on peut voir le bateau qui passe dans l'air avec les filets tendus.

Encore, parfois, on peut voir, le noyé bercé entre deux eaux, le corps lumineux.

Encore, parfois, on peut voir le violier comme une croix dans son Golgotha interminable.

Encore, parfois, on peut voir les pirates accrochés à la quille, et le capitaine pendu au grand mât dans la haute mer.

Encore on peut voir à la lumière d'un éclair le timonier pâle, les barbes au vent.

Encore on peut voir à la lumière d'un éclair la morte nue, les seins gonflés.

Encore on peut voir à la lumière d'un éclair le cheval du rapt qui se perd au loin.

Encore, parfois, on peut voir dans les nuits de lune, la main qui flotte.

Mais la pêche de sirènes, les cheveux pris dans les filets, n'a pas été revue et en vain nous attendons.

Nous avons salué toutes les vagues, nous avons regardé attentivement, nous avons agité nos chapeaux et nos mouchoirs, nous avons joué leurs seins aux dés, sur le pont de milliers de bateaux. Tout, inutilement. Les complices de l'aube entendirent les fleurs en voyage, entendirent la marche de la lumière polaire, et une autre fois encore la marche du héros vers l'âge de pierre.

Mais personne ne verra le supplice des sirènes.

En vain vous levez les doigts, montrant chaque pli de la mer ou chaque tremblement dans les nuages.

I tell you, she is better hidden than the night.

A bird, solitary as the sea, flies off slowly, perhaps because of your cries.

It flies off slowly, I say, to the wonders of its own slumber. It flies off carrying with it the meaning of evening.

Not for you the panorama of the emerging secret.

What do you know of encounters in eternity?

I tell you again, she is better hidden than the night at mid-day.

Uselessly, we get under way on our joyous exploration, and for the impassive catch barely lit by the sea's inner light, barely swayed by silence or solitude.

* * *

Who was the killer?

Before the judge lies the body of a woman like the mummy of the most beautiful of the Pharaoh's wives.

Cry out, accusers.

In vain the judge examines the eyes of those present. No eye present matches the shape of the wound that can still be seen bleeding on the bare chest.

A violent gust of wind closes all eyelids. The judge flushes with anger.

—Gentlemen, who heard the gunshot?

Did no-one see a shadow fleeing through the window? Did no-one see a light in the middle of the night?

All eyes return to the giant man eating fireflies in the garden.

Through his transparent body something like a hidden dagger or a lily could be seen, but the composure of the alleged criminal sowed doubt in the minds of his accusers.

Two tears roll down his cheeks.

—He's the one, he's the one, some shout.

—It's not him, it's not him, shout others.

A roll of drums comes down from the sky as though a rain of stones were falling upon the moon.

The accused remains unmoved. With large eyes, without the slightest flicker of a lash, even at the moment when he feels a crown beginning to form around his brow.

Je vous le dis, elle est plus cachée que la nuit.

Un oiseau solitaire comme la mer s'éloigne lentement, peut-être à cause de vos cris.

S'éloigne lentement, je dis, vers les merveilles de son propre sommeil. S'éloigne emportant le sens du soir.

Ce n'est pas pour vous le panorama du secret naissant.

Que savez-vous des rencontres dans l'éternité?

Je vous répète elle est plus cachée que la nuit au milieu du jour.

Inutilement nous appareillons vers l'heureuse exploration, et vers les pêches impossibles à peines illuminées par les lumières internes de la mer, à peine bercée par le silence ou la solitude.

* * *

Qui a été l'assassin?

Devant le juge est placé le cadavre de la femme, comme la momie de la plus belle pharaonne.

Criez, accusateurs.

Inutilement le juge scrute les yeux des assistants. La forme d'aucun œil présent ne correspond à la forme de la blessure qu'on voit encore saignante sur la poitrine nue.

Une rafale violente ferme toutes les paupières. Le juge rougit de colère.

—Messieurs, qui a entendu le coup de feu?

Personne n'a vu une ombre fuir par la fenêtre? Personne n'a vu une lumière au milieu de la nuit?

Tous les yeux se tournent vers l'homme géant qui mangeait les lucioles dans le jardin.

A travers la transparence de son corps on voyait quelque chose comme un poignard ou un lys caché, mais la tranquillité du présumé criminel semait le doute dans la conscience de ses accusateurs.

Deux larmes coulent le long de ses joues.

—C'est lui, c'est lui, crient quelques-uns.

—Ce n'est pas lui, ce n'est pas lui, crient d'autres.

Un roulement de tambours descend par le ciel, comme s'il tombait une pluie de pierres sur la lune.

L'accusé demeure imperturbable. Les grands yeux fixes, sans le moindre battement des cils, même au moment où il sent une couronne qui commence à pousser autour de son front.

Everyone looks towards the street. The procession that erupted from the triumphant explosion passes by. Banners unfurled like the wind. Everyone watches, but he does not even blink an eye.

—Get the killer. Get the killer!

When the mob lunged for him, a thousand raised fists struck a marble statue gazing fixedly at the horizon.

Then on the horizon a comet appeared, with a long mantle of fireflies, and began to rise through the sky which received it with open arms.

A few moments later, a window opened deep within the same horizon, and the bride with her beautiful drowsy eyes came out to watch the comet, trying to decipher the omen, perhaps a sorrowful one, that its presence amongst mankind announced. What magical signs does the bride make with her sky-white hands? On her right hand she wears a perfect diamond, from which a fountain of water begins to flow, running tamely towards us.

Suddenly a deafening clamour rises into the air.

—To the guillotine! The guillotine, the guillotine!

Moments later, when the fateful blade had severed the marble head of the accused before the bloodthirsty mob, an enormous jet of light spurted unceasingly from his neck.

At the same moment there was a terrifying quake in the sky. Stars shattered into a thousand pieces, planets burst into flames, fragments of moons flew past, red-hot coals leaped from volcanoes on other worlds and sometimes landed, sizzling, in the bulging eyes of men.

The mob fled in terror.

Some hid below ground, crying for help, while others fell to their knees beating their breasts and begging forgiveness, arms raised to the heavens.

The jet of light kept flowing from the neck of the executed man on the gibbet.

* * *

Amidst the catastrophe and general confusion, two arms stronger than a hundred seas tightened around my throat.

—Isolde, Isolde, is that you?

—How many years we have been apart.

Tous regardent vers les rues. On voit passer le cortège jailli de l'explosion triomphale. Les drapeaux dépliés comme le vent. Tous regardent mais lui ne bouge même pas les yeux.

—À l'assassin, à l'assassin!

Quand la foule s'élança sur lui mille poings levés se heurtèrent contre une statue de marbre qui regardait fixement l'horizon.

Alors à l'horizon apparut une comète avec un long manteau de lucioles et commença à se lever sur le ciel qui la recevait bras ouverts.

Quelques minutes après une fenêtre s'ouvrit au fond du même horizon et la fiancée apparut avec ses beaux yeux endormis, regardant la comète et tâchant de deviner le présage, peut-être douloureux, qu'annonçait sa présence parmi les hommes. Quels signes magiques fait la fiancée avec ses mains blanches comme le ciel? Elle a, à sa main droite un diamant parfait, duquel commence à couler une source d'eau qui court docile vers nous.

Soudain une clameur assourdissante s'éleva dans les airs.

—À la guillotine! La guillotine, la guillotine!

Quelques moments plus tard, quand devant la foule assoiffée de sang le couteau fatal trancha la tête de marbre de l'accusé, un immense jet de lumière jaillit de son cou interminablement.

Au même instant il y eût dans le ciel un épouvantable tremblement. Les étoiles se brisèrent en mille morceaux, les planètes prirent feu, des fragments de lunes volèrent, des charbons rouges sautèrent des volcans des autres astres et vinrent parfois se clouer pétillants dans les yeux désorbités des hommes.

La multitude, effrayée, prenait la fuite.

Les uns se cachaient sous terre en demandant secours et d'autres tombaient à genoux se frappant la poitrine et implorant pardon les bras levés vers le ciel.

Le jet de lumière continuait à couler du cou de l'exécuté sur la plate-forme de la mort.

* * *

Au milieu de la catastrophe et de la confusion générale deux bras plus puissants que cent mers étreignirent ma gorge.

—Iseult, Iseult, c'est toi?

—Combien d'années nous avons été loin l'un de l'autre.

—It took carnage like this for us to meet again.

—You, tree of wisdom, with mature eyes at dream's door and that elephant-like gait with the feet of an idol.

—Show me your breasts.

—Always waiting for the age of wonders, like the magician's dove.

—Let me kiss your breasts.

The imprisoned angel breaks his chains and flies into the air, pursued in vain by a few unskilled shotguns.

Powerful, solitary, night begins to fall once more. The snakes illuminated by the storm bound forward chasing the liberated angel, who is impossible to catch.

Isolde clings to me, embedded in my arms.

In the lightning-forge hammering can be heard, as the storm shapes the crown for my kingly head.

How many will be blinded by this all too brilliant crown

Countless are those who, upon seeing it, behold the final vision of their lives. The handsome giant in his final agony above the sea, asks only to look upon it once more, so he might come back to life or die in peace.

Numerous are the visions engraved upon it as if on a frieze. The body of a woman may be seen there, burning in the fire rising from her own flesh and there is no way of extinguishing the flames.

And so many other visions. Like that of dwarfs flying past, carrying on their shoulders the coffin of a Titan.

And that of the island, snatched away by the wind, falling onto the city.

And that of lightning interwoven with storm rains.

And that of palm trees bent beneath the wheels of the hurricane.

And that of the mountain of clouds that lingers for so long that sweet greenery begins to grow upon it.

And that of the bitter night when someone is dying.

I believe that the moment has come to think of the night when we ourselves will die.

Isolde, I love you, and through all the others, I have only ever sought to love you more.

Bitter is the night and deep the abyss where your arms cast me. I fall, my hands despairing, like a Niagara irretrievably lost.

The foam splashes my face before I reach the bottom.

—Il a fallu une hécatombe semblable pour se rencontrer de nouveau.

—Toi, arbre de la sagesse, avec les yeux mûrs à la porte du rêve, et cette démarche d'éléphant aux pieds d'idole.

—Montre-moi tes seins.

—Toujours attendant l'âge des merveilles comme la colombe du mage.

—Donne-moi à baiser tes seins.

L'ange prisonnier rompt ses chaînes et vole dans les airs, poursuivi en vain par quelques fusils inexperts.

Puissante et solitaire tombe à nouveau la nuit. Les serpents illuminés de la tempête courent par bonds derrière l'ange libéré impossible à attraper.

Iseult se serre contre moi, s'incruste dans mes bras.

Dans la forge des éclairs on entend les martèlements de la bourrasque que façonne la couronne pour ma tête de roi.

Combien d'aveugles aura fait cette couronne trop brillante.

Innombrables sont ceux qui en la voyant contemplent la dernière vision de leur vie. Le précieux géant qui agonise sur la mer demande seulement à la regarder pour revenir à la vie ou mourir tranquille.

Nombreuses sont les visions gravées sur elles comme sur une frise. On y voit le corps d'une femme brûlant dans l'incendie qui s'élève de ses propres chairs et il est impossible d'éteindre les flammes.

Et tant d'autres visions. Comme celles de nains qui passent au vol portant sur le dos le cercueil d'un Titan.

Et celle de l'île arrachée par le vent qui tombe sur la ville.

Et celle de la foudre entretissée dans la pluie de la bourrasque.

Et celle des palmiers courbés sous les roues de l'ouragan.

Et celle de la montagne de nuages qui s'arrête si longtemps qu'il commence à pousser sur elle une douce végétation.

Et celle de la nuit amère où quelqu'un meurt.

Je crois qu'il est arrivé le moment de penser à la nuit où nous mourrons.

Iseult, je t'aime et à travers toutes les autres j'ai seulement cherché à t'aimer davantage.

Amère est la nuit et profonde l'abîme où tes bras me jetèrent. Je tombe les mains désespérées comme un Niagara irrémissiblement perdu.

L'écume éclabousse ma figure avant de toucher le fond.

Le bruit assourdit mes oreilles, rebondit dans mon cerveau avant que mes chairs ne se brisent en morceaux tout au fond.

The noise deafens my ears, reverberates in my brain, before my flesh is dashed to pieces at the very bottom.

I keep smiling nonetheless, hopeful that at any moment my body will feel lighter than air.

Or that a lasso might fall from some unknown star, take hold of me, lift me up at the very moment before I touch the ground.

—Isolde, there you have it; the conduct of a perfect man.

The wind rocks me in all directions. Below, the gaze of men tethers me to their earthly fear, on a sad plain with an isolated house visible in the distance, and a plume of smoke trying to lift the house into the sky.

The house where the crime took place can never be freed from its patch of land. And yet, although the spectacle has become rather dismal, the night is brighter than ever, there is not a single empty space in all the heavens. And all this to see what?

The beautiful woman's throat takes the form of a song.

And she will sing; she will sing, certain that I am not about to die. She will sing despite the season's waning, despite the night rolling down from the mountains, despite the difficult terrain. She will sing.

And the child will stop crying over his little white boat. And a very fine star will appear above his head, deep in the recess, beyond his sensitive ears, on the true reef of his last dream.

Perhaps we will hear the voice in a vast song because the sea is spread out over several player-pianos and occasionally surrenders to its own instincts.

Then comes the hour of transfiguration. The sea sweats and writhes in intimate pain. Each wave turns into an angel and flies away.

Woe unto him who dares raise a hand to the sea!

You do not know this, and so I tell you now: by night, when no-one is watching, the sea turns into a great monument and they say that at the top, there stands a solemn statue of itself.

No-one will ever know the truth of it, nor the number of mistakes that each man makes at every moment of his life.

Upon how many errors does each human invention rest?

These inventions finer than an electric spark, or a woman's legs. Here all wise men bow, here prophets kneel, here the cock crows and where its song ends a landscape is born, as everyone knows. Afterwards only the hands of castaways can be seen clinging to the waves, and a bottle that floats away to tell their tale of so much distress.

Cependant je souris encore espérant que d'un instant à l'autre mon corps puisse se sentir plus léger que l'air.

Ou qu'un lasso tombe d'une étoile inconnue et me prenne et me soulève juste au moment où j'allais toucher le sol.

—Iseult, voilà l'attitude de l'homme parfait.

Le vent me berce dans tous les sens. En bas les regards des hommes m'attachent à leur frayeur terrestre dans une plaine triste dans laquelle on voit une maison isolée là-bas loin, et une fumée qui essaye d'élever la maison au ciel.

La maison du crime jamais ne pourra se décoller de son morceau de région. Pourtant, bien que le spectacle soit devenu maintenant assez lamentable, la nuit est plus brillante que jamais, il n'y a pas une place libre dans tout le ciel. Et cela, pour voir quoi?

La gorge de la belle femme a la forme d'une chanson.

Et elle chantera; elle chantera certaine que je ne mourrai pas encore. Elle chantera malgré la saison trop avancée, malgré la nuit qui roule en bas des montagnes, malgré les difficultés du terrain. Elle chantera.

Et l'enfant cessera de pleurer sur son petit navire blanc. Et une étoile très fine paraîtra au-dessus de sa tête, au fond de l'alcôve au-delà de ses oreilles sensibles, sur le récif véritable de son dernier rêve.

Peut-être entendrons-nous la voix dans un chant énorme parce que la mer est étendue sur plusieurs pianolas et elle s'abandonne parfois à ses propres instincts.

Alors arrive l'heure de la transfiguration. La mer sue et se tord d'une intime douleur. Chaque vague devient ange et s'envole.

Malheur à celui qui ose lever la main sur la mer!

Vous ne le savez pas, c'est pourquoi je vous le dis: pendant la nuit, quand personne ne la regarde, la mer devient un grand monument et l'on dit qu'en haut se dresse, solennelle sa propre statue.

Personne ne saura jamais quelle est la vérité, et non plus le nombre d'erreurs que manie chaque homme à tous les instants de sa vie.

Sur quelle quantité d'erreurs repose chaque invention de l'homme?

Ces inventions plus belles qu'une étincelle électrique et les jambes une femme. Ici s'inclinent tous les savants, ici s'agenouillent les prophètes, ici chante le coq et là où finit sa chanson naît un paysage, comme tout monde sait. Après on voit seulement les mains des naufragés accrochées aux vagues et une bouteille qui flotte et s'éloigne pour raconter l'histoire de tant d'angoisse.

Isolde, if only you knew!

The sky has changed seven times. And it will change again because of the sea. Because the sea has turned into a balloon, slipped its moorings and drifted away into the sky.

What do you gain by aiming your cannons and ringing your bells?

On the horizon, the sun sets, reaches out a hand, and barely looks at us from just behind its five fingers, spread out like the spokes of a wheel. What can we do?

Above the deserted countryside an egg falls from a passing eagle that was unsure of its destination. This will be a fertile field for many years to come and perhaps a great capital will arise there.

Telescopes are raised and become lost in eternity. The sky strips off. Meteorites and lightning-flashes pass beyond the Milky Way, the ceremonial procession of comets advances and no-one fears the wrath of God any more.

The sky strips off and there we can see the dying eyes of the one who thought he had created everything.

The sky strips off and the nocturnal ghost that brings daily refreshments to the stars is revealed.

The sky strips off and the cavern of candelabras appears; in its centre sleeps the woman of flesh and blood that we all know, wrapped in her tresses.

Hypnotised zebras gallop by and windows can be seen that open onto the darkness stuck to the night like parasites.

Ah, if only you knew! I am hidden inside your shadow. I am the newborn tree inside your eyes. I am the child, barefoot like a statue, calling out from the shipwreck amidst impassive reflections.

I am the spectre that leaves, guided by its doves, those doves full of wisdom that feed off the light from swaying lanterns.

Here I am, weary and terrible, more terrible than the doomed ship, which sails howling through the sky, and dies quietly like a man or like a dog feeling for the first time the weight of the skeleton beneath its flesh.

Ah, if you could see it! When the maternal womb opens like a cage and the woman raises her arms to infinity, offering all flights yet to come.

If you could see it. The trembling roofs before they rise up forever. The roofs that will leave for who knows where, laden with clouds.

Iseult, si tu savais!

Le ciel a changé sept fois. Et il changera encore à cause de la mer. Parce que la mer est devenue un ballon et lâcha ses amarres, et s'en alla par le ciel.

Que gagnez-vous à pointer vos canons et à sonner vos cloches?

À l'horizon le soleil se couche, il tend la main et nous regarde à peine derrière ses cinq doigts écartés comme les rayons d'une roue. Que pouvons-nous faire?

Sur la campagne déserte tombe l'œuf d'une aigle qui passait en volant sans savoir où diriger ses pas. Celui-là sera le champ de la fécondité pendant plusieurs d'années, et peut-être là même naîtra une grande capitale.

Les télescopes se lèvent et se perdent dans l'éternité. Le ciel se déshabille. Des aérolithes et des éclairs passent au-delà de la voie lactée, le cortège cérémonieux des comètes avance et personne ne craint plus la colère de Dieu.

Le ciel se déshabille, et l'on voit les yeux agonisants de celui qui croyait avoir tout créé.

Le ciel se déshabille et on voit le fantôme nocturne qui porte aux astres la nourriture quotidienne.

Le ciel se déshabille et on voit la grotte de candélabres au milieu de laquelle dort la femme de chair que nous connaissons tous, enveloppée dans ses cheveux.

Les zèbres hypnotisés passent au galop et l'on voit les fenêtres qui s'ouvrent dans l'obscurité comme des parasites collés à la nuit.

Ah si tu savais! Je suis caché en dedans de ton ombre. Je suis l'arbre nouveau-né en dedans de tes yeux. Je suis l'enfant aux pieds nus comme une statue qui crie dans le naufrage parmi les reflets impossibles.

Je suis le spectre qui s'éloigne, guidé par ses colombes, ces colombes pleines de savoir qui se nourrissent de la lumière des lanternes titubantes.

Me voici fatigué et terrible, plus terrible que le bateau condamné, qui s'éloigne hurlant par le ciel et meurt doucement comme un homme ou comme un chien quand ils sentent, pour la première fois, le poids de son squelette sous la chair.

Ah si tu voyais! Quand le ventre maternel s'ouvre comme une cage et la femme lève les bras vers l'infini offrant tous les envols futurs.

Si tu voyais. Les toits tremblant avant de s'élever pour toujours. Les toits qui s'en iront on ne sait pas où, avec leurs charges de nuages.

If you could see now the insect that jumps at the contact of two vindictive cables and can assume the form of a man, as far as the attentive observer can tell.

And the unconsciousness of night surrounded by a deep channel, the unconsciousness of trees that frequently clash. How many times have I seen them tug at each other's hair, and hurl insults over a bird.

In the face of such mysteries, in the face of such occult powers, the unconsciousness of the sea, which could cleave in two at any moment, is an incredible thing. But you know the day will come when they will be touched by grace like the mountains. And then each will have a halo.

Then we will see the young girls as they come out of school, their braids caught in the wind, flying lightly towards the kite and the bells of joy and death that await them at the entrance to the volcano.

We will see the statue wandering over the houses, washed by rain like a warrior's wounds. We will see the transformations of silence and the ecstasies of those watching the sunset play, and then the star twinkling in the breeze.

But only a dying man will see a flower waving its hands inside the womb of the beloved woman. And afterwards he will drink death down in a single gulp.

The woman might walk away leave, sweeping life aside with her skirts; she might wait naked above the night, all her beauty set free.

She might lean over the balcony of her splendour, she might walk around with her white shoulders full of nights, not bothered by the rain falling on her bones, the rain where hanged men can seldom be strung up. But she scents sadness, she hears the voice of the grave and opens her mouth to bite into death.

The man approaching is blindfolded and raises a hymn or an aquatic plant in his hand.

All the bridges collapse and the queen cannot pass, the queen whose mind is perfumed by her thoughts, the queen with blue eyes smelling of the sea.

Fever escapes through her pores, and her five senses perish at the very threshold of mystery.

Only the heart's breast keeps on living, surrounded by its vassals, with all their myths concerning statues. It keeps on living and watching like a bulging eye, disobeying the orders of the Creator, who reigns deep within his dream.

Si tu voyais maintenant l'insecte qui jaillit au contact de deux câbles vindicatifs et qui peut prendre même la forme d'un homme pour l'œil qui regarde avec attention.

Et l'inconscience de la nuit entourée d'un canal profond, l'inconscience des arbres qui se battent fréquemment. Combien de fois je les ai vu se tirer les cheveux et s'insulter pour un oiseau.

Devant de tels mystères, devant de telles forces occultes l'inconscience de la mer qui pourrait soudain se couper en deux est quelque chose d'incroyable. Mais tu sais qu'il arrivera un jour où ils seront touchés par la grâce, comme les montagnes. Et alors chacun aura une auréole.

Alors nous verrons les jeunes filles qui sortent du collège en un vol léger les tresses au vent vers le cerf-volant et les cloches de joie et de mort qui les attendent à l'entrée du volcan.

Nous verrons la statue qui se promène sur les maisons lavées par la pluie comme les blessures du guerrier. Nous verrons les transformations du silence et les extases de celui qui regarde les jeux du couchant, et puis l'étoile clignotante dans le courant d'air.

Mais seul l'homme qui agonise verra une fleur agitant les mains à l'intérieur du ventre de la femme aimée. Et après il boira la mort d'un trait.

La femme pourra s'éloigner balayant la vie avec ses jupes, elle pourra l'attendre nue, au-dessus de la nuit, avec toute sa beauté en liberté.

Elle pourra se pencher au balcon de sa splendeur, elle pourra se promener avec les épaules blanches pleines de nocturnes, sans prendre garde à la pluie qui tombe sur ses os, la pluie où l'on peut rarement attacher les pendus. Mais elle flaire la tristesse, elle entend la voix des tombeaux et ouvre la bouche pour mordre la mort.

L'homme qui s'approche a les yeux ligotés et lève un hymne ou une plante aquatique dans la main.

Tous les ponts s'écroulent et la reine ne peut pas passer, la reine au cerveau parfumé par ses pensées, la reine aux yeux bleus à l'odeur de mer.

Par ses pores s'échappe la fièvre et ses cinq sens meurent à la porte même du mystère.

Seul le sein du cœur continue à vivre, entouré de ses vassaux avec tous ses mythes de statue. Il continue à vivre et à regarder comme un œil désorbité, sans obéir aux ordres du créateur qui trône au fond de son rêve.

How many sacks of gold does the miser hoard in his cavern to buy that breast, which will float until the end of time in his barrel of memories!

Perhaps a clumsy child, lips poisoned by chimeras, will bite him now that so many hands are extended his way. Perhaps, older than his years, he will fight a fierce battle for the sex one can only guess at beneath the shadow's clothing.

She is the ghost with transparent skin who, instead of a face, has a circular void between her hair and neck.

Flee, delicate child, with your crown of caresses on your head. Flee, I tell you, to the polar caverns and sing while the legendary beauty listens to the sound of shells racing behind her.

* * *

With nets extended from breast to breast, others could wait.

During the night, the sweet quake hides in undersea caverns. There the pearl-diver descends, and sometimes he has found the legendary maiden there, lying upon the waters, her arms bound.

Then he climbs back up the ladder suspended from the night and vanishes into the region where there are birds of augury.

From the highest rock he can toss a rope to the woman crucified amongst her plunder and lift her to the treetops, where those who still bear memories of the Flood climb anxiously.

Run and dry yourselves at the mouth of the volcano which will soon raise its banners in triumph.

Earthly child, when you try to reconcile wings with your thermal eyes, you forget the flowering of the inner labyrinth, you forget the glowing cavern of the possessed.

The volcano can remind you of whatever you forget and will throw you a flower in its memory, then you will see the whole universe pass before you, just as the savage standing on the mountain watches the hurricane, or the river full of uprooted trees, pass by.

The woman we all know will drift away from you along the shores of wandering stars, with the weight of her hair on her shoulders she will drift away beneath a moon swollen by gluttony or perhaps by the occasional rain of eternal snows. The woman will drift away with a precious corpse under her arm and she will suddenly see an island of violent colours coming towards her.

Combien de sacs d'or amoncelle l'avare dans sa caverne pour acheter ce sein qui flottera jusqu'à la fin des siècles dans sa barrique pleine de souvenirs!

Peut-être un enfant inexpert aux lèvres empoisonnées de chimères va le mordre maintenant que tant de mains se tendent vers lui. Peut-être il va livrer une bataille acharnée, en dehors de son âge, pour le sexe qu'on devine se promenait sous les robes d'ombres.

Elle est le fantôme à la peau transparente qui n'a pas de figure, mais un vide rond entre les cheveux et le cou.

Fuis, enfant délicat, avec ta couronne de caresses sur la tête. Fuis, je te dis, aux cavernes du Pôle et chante tandis que la belle fabuleuse, écoute le bruit des obus qui courent derrière elle.

* * *

Les filets tendus de sein à sein, d'autres ont pu attendre.

Pendant la nuit le précieux tremblement se cache dans les grottes marines. Là descend le chercheur de perles et parfois il a trouvé couchée sur les eaux la jeune fabuleuse, les bras liés.

Alors il gravit à nouveau l'échelle qui pend de la nuit et se perd dans la zone des oiseaux devins.

Du plus haut rocher il peut lancer une corde à la femme crucifiée dans ses dépouilles et la lever jusqu'au sommet des arbres où grimpent angoissés ceux qui gardent encore le souvenir du déluge.

Courrez-vous sécher à la bouche du volcan qui bientôt lèvera ses drapeaux en signe de triomphe.

Enfant terrestre quand tu essayes de concilier les ailes avec tes yeux thermaux, tu oublies les florescences du labyrinthe interne, tu oublies la caverne lumineuse des possédés.

Le volcan saura te rappeler ce que tu oublies et te lancera une fleur à la mémoire et alors tu verras passer devant toi tout l'univers comme le sauvage debout sur la montagne regarde passer l'ouragan ou le fleuve plein d'arbres déracinés.

La femme que nous connaissons tous s'éloignera de toi le long des rives des astres errants, avec la charge de sa chevelure sur les épaules, s'éloignera sous une lune qui se gonfle par gloutonnerie ou peut-être à cause de la pluie périodique des neiges éternelles. S'éloignera la femme avec le précieux cadavre sous le bras et elle verra soudain venir vers elle une île aux couleurs violentes.

Her majestic hair will fall into the sea, amidst the age-old seaweed. She will be clothed in madness, glowing with her own light, and will be like a silk lampshade watched by a dying man.

Meanwhile, the other, in his prison of science, will not be able to raise his eyes without seeing on every book, or on every microscope, the statue with enormous breasts and a polished belly, bringing his own heart to life.

This is the statue with living alcohol gushing forth from its pores and cascading down to its shackled feet.

And this game that you believed was the game of life is nothing but the game of death.

Here is man on top of woman from the beginning of the world. Man on top of woman forever like the stone over a tomb.

You are none other than death on top of death.

Consider the last spasms of that woman who is dying in death.

And so, you go through life locked inside death.

—Isolde, in vain do you sigh at night, in vain do you cry out my name when I can no longer hear, when a bloody sweat covers my ears, when the sky empties into my retina. Every man is a coward. Do not believe in the exceptional things that your dream, fallen from other less tangible stars, paints for you. The mystic is a man of dread, a man who does not want to be alone, the one who, from fear of loneliness, wishes he were two.

Ah, if only you knew!

What would I not give to silence them with their bluish voices and shatter the forms and colours of their eternal or fleeting feelings, always sweet, too sweet for the palate of an infinite castaway.

Events rank higher than the human voice. The phenomenon now condensed into a marble banner is much more important than your arts, your artifices, or your artfulness.

Sheet music is a seedbed with no destiny. No future forests will grow there, look at it and you will see that it barely marks out a temporary vineyard.

The sea brings the sensitive coffin to the threshold of your house, perhaps even to your bedside, so that you can shut yourself in with your precious hysteria and your howls, those filthy howls, filthy as the tears of the algebraic proof of pain.

Shut yourself inside it so that the seed cannot escape your womb, for it could be a piano with its twilight microbes, a piano with a turbulent soul leaping like the mine on the sea floor.

Sa chevelure auguste tombera sur la mer parmi les algues millénaires. Elle s'habillera de folie avec toute sa lumière propre et sera comme l'abat-jour de soie que regarde le moribond.

Entre temps l'autre dans sa prison de science ne pourra pas lever les yeux sans voir sur chaque livre, sur chaque microscope la statue aux seins énormes et au ventre poli qui anime son propre cœur.

Celle-là est la statue de l'alcool vivant, qui jaillit de ses pores et tombe en cascade jusqu'aux pieds enchaînés.

Et ce jeu que vous avez cru qui était le jeu de la vie, n'était que le jeu de la mort.

Voici l'homme sur la femme depuis le commencement du monde. L'homme sur la femme éternellement comme la pierre sur le tombeau.

Vous n'êtes pas autre chose que la mort sur la mort.

Contemple le geste de spasme de celle qui se meurt dans la mort.

Ainsi donc tu traverses la vie enfermée dans la mort.

—Iseult, en vain tu soupires dans la nuit, en vain tu cries mon nom quand je n'entends plus, quand une sueur de sang me couvre les oreilles, quand le ciel se vide dans ma rétine. Tout homme est un lâche. Ne crois pas aux exceptionnels que te peint le rêve tombé d'autres astres moins palpables. Le mystique est l'homme de l'épouvante, est l'homme qui ne veut pas être seul, est celui qui veut être deux par peur de la solitude.

Ah si tu savais!

Que ne donnerais-je pas pour les faire taire avec leur voix bleutée, et leur briser les formes et les couleurs du sentiment éternel ou passager, toujours doux, trop doux pour le palais d'un naufragé infini.

Les événements sont au-dessus de la voix humaine. Le phénomène qui se condense aujourd'hui en un drapeau de marbre, est beaucoup plus important que tes arts, tes artifices et tes artisteries.

Le papier de musique est une pépinière sans destin. De là ne jailliront pas les forêts futures, regarde-le et tu verras qu'il marque à peine un vignoble momentané.

La mer te porte le cercueil sensible jusqu'au seuil de ta maison, peut-être même jusqu'au bord de ton lit, pour que tu t'enfermes en lui, avec ta précieuse hystérie et tes hurlements, ces hurlements sales, sales comme les larmes de la démonstration algébrique de la douleur.

Enferme-toi en lui, et que la semence de ton ventre ne sorte pas car elle pourrait être un piano avec ses microbes de crépuscule, un piano d'âme turbulente, qui saute comme la mine au fond de l'eau.

Raise your arms, woman, and beg forgiveness of the creature that is cradled between your legs and wants nothing to do with the light from your little household lanterns.

Blow, blow and extinguish those illusory lights with a magic word. Blow and extinguish the statue that is already about to ask directions, that would like to know how the weather will be tomorrow.

Lower the finger with which you were going to point to the destiny on offer, to your experiences of shadow, while a ship is sinking and leaping from tornado to tornado, from abyss to abyss beneath the black sky.

Better to use your time rippling your hair like a simple sea that listens to its timid birds as they pass through the evening.

Keep your night-time lectures for the festive crowd, leaning on the harbour railings. Keep for them the ritual of your breasts that can no longer be held up.

Soon the king's coach must carry you off with your womb and your legs, your cometary gaze, through the applauding crowd. What more do you want?

The palace has grand staircases that lead who knows where. Columns hold up arches, from planet to planet, and in every vase there are severed heads.

Behind the bars eternity can be seen sleeping in indescribable serenity. What more do you want?

This is your destiny. Leave each to their own freedom, which lies at the beginning or end of the flight, like a shelter or a harbour. And now keep quiet.

The dying man purses his lips so that the last bird will not escape to sing its song on other rocks.

Everything obeys the cadence of a voice that falls from who knows where.

That is the destiny of the magnetic butterfly.

That is the skeleton patiently awaiting its time, hidden in the shadows. The final skeleton that will play chess beneath its earthly house, while its hats live on other people's streets.

And you may weep because such is the tree's horoscope.

Hide your caresses in the caverns of polar birds where the man drives stalactites into his eyes and the woman runs leaping between icebergs.

Lève les bras, femme, et demande pardon à la créature qui se berce entre tes jambes et ne veut rien savoir de la lumière de tes petites lanternes domestiques.

Souffle, souffle et éteins ces lumières de chimère avec une parole magique. Souffle et éteins la statue qui va déjà demander le chemin, qui déjà veut savoir le temps qu'il fera demain.

Abaisse le doigt avec lequel tu allais signaler le destin offert, tes expériences d'ombre tandis qu'un bateau est en train de sombrer et saute de trombe en trombe, d'abîme en abîme, sous le ciel noir.

Emploie mieux ton temps à onduler tes cheveux comme une mer innocente qui écoute ses oiseaux flasques traversant le soir.

Garde pour la foule en fête creuse, accoudée sur les balustrades du port, tes leçons nocturnes. Garde pour elle le cérémonial de tes seins qui ne peuvent plus tenir.

Bientôt doit t'emporter le carrosse du roi avec ton ventre et tes jambes, avec ton regard de comète à travers la multitude qui t'applaudit. Que veux-tu de plus?

Le palais a de grands escaliers qui finissent on ne sait où. Les colonnes soutiennent des ogives, de planète à planète, et dans toutes les vasques il y a des têtes coupées.

Au-delà des grilles on voit l'éternité endormie avec une placidité indescriptible. Que veux-tu de plus?

Celui-là est ton destin. Laisse à chacun sa liberté qui est au commencement ou à la fin du vol comme une branche ou un port. Et maintenant tais-toi.

Le moribond serre les lèvres, pour que l'oiseau définitif ne fuie pas chanter sa romance sur d'autres rochers.

Tout obéit à la cadence d'une voix: personne ne sait d'où elle tombe.

Voilà le destin du papillon magnétique.

Voilà le squelette attendant patiemment son heure, caché dans les ombres. Le squelette final qui jouera aux échecs sous sa maison de terre, tandis que ses chapeaux vivent dans les rues d'autrui.

Et vous pouvez pleurer parce que semblable est l'horoscope de l'arbre.

Cachez les caresses dans les cavernes des oiseaux polaires où l'homme se cloue des stalactites dans les yeux, et la femme court en sautant parmi les icebergs.

—Isolde, the hurricane is already here, laying waste the cemetery of gazes, the hurricane is already here, with the speed of planets hurled to their fates.

Let us hide in the deepest catacombs and carve our names there in the soft stone by the niche where we are to lie for eternity.

There the curious of tomorrow will find our skulls and our bones entwined.

Time's brow bleeds in the restless darkness of night, bleeds, ripped by mountains of thorns.

What does it matter!

On the terrace of the highest peak my throat once swallowed all the thunder from the sky, and my fingers stroked the lightning's back, while the sun, regrouped its forces behind the night and prepared for the next day's attack.

Do you hear the sound of the waves colliding because of the darkness?

Do not fear. Let us go. It is death's sailing ship. The beloved monster comes closer and licks at our hands. The earth is gentle and soft as the mattress of eternity.

The bride invites us to the celebration of her womb. Her kiss tastes of cosmic lips and she must carry us further than anyone could have thought possible.

Now you pass by and I see the geological tree-like forms inside your glowing heart, that mark your age on earth.

Do you hear the sound of waves colliding with the night?

Do you hear the sound of waves banging their heads together? Now you pass by and are lost in landscapes that were impregnable yesterday, you travel roads that are still alive but as ambiguous as ever.

Soon you will encounter the ghost that cries out: "Every man for himself", and flings its feelings and memories overboard so as to lighten its load.

You will encounter someone who discards his years like ballast from a balloon and then sings of his folly with the voice of a shackled and satisfied bridegroom.

You will encounter the man who knows everything, the hideous man who ignores nothing, who always has a ready answer, ripe words on the boughs of his lips, the man who has studied the flower's innards, who knows the past, the present and the future and the genealogy of every wave.

—Iseult, déjà vient l'ouragan ravageant le cimetière des regards, déjà vient l'ouragan à la vitesse des planètes lancées au destin.

Cachons-nous dans les plus profondes catacombes et là gravons notre nom dans les pierres sensitives près de la niche où nous devons nous coucher pour l'éternité.

Là les curieux de demain trouveront nos crânes et nos os mêlés.

Le front du temps saigne dans l'obscurité sans repos de la nuit, saigne déchiré par des montagnes d'épines.

Qu'importe!

Sur la terrasse du dernier sommet ma gorge avalait une fois tous les tonnerres du ciel, et mes doigts caressèrent l'échine des éclairs, tandis que le soleil derrière la nuit rassemblait les restes de ses troupes et se préparait pour l'attaque du lendemain.

Entends-tu le bruit des vagues qui se heurtent à cause de l'obscurité.

Ne crains pas. Allons-nous-en. C'est le voilier de la mort. Le monstre aimé s'approche et vient lécher nos mains. La terre est douce et molle comme le matelas de l'éternité.

L'épouse nous invite à la fête de ses entrailles. Son baiser a le goût des lèvres cosmiques, et elle doit nous emporter plus loin de ce que personne peut soupçonner.

Maintenant tu passes et je vois au-dedans de ton cœur illuminé les arborescences géologiques qui marquent ton âge sur la terre.

Entends-tu le bruit des vagues qui se heurtent contre la nuit?

Entends-tu le bruit des vagues qui se cassent la tête? Maintenant tu passes et tu te perds dans les paysages hier inexpugnables, tu t'en vas par les chemins encore vivants et aussi équivoques que toujours.

Bientôt tu rencontreras le fantôme qui crie: «sauve qui peut»; et jette ses sentiments et ses souvenirs par-dessus bord pour se faire plus léger.

Tu rencontreras aussi celui qui lance ses années comme le lest d'un ballon et après chante son inconscience avec une voix de fiancé enchaîné et satisfait.

Tu rencontreras l'homme qui sait tout, l'homme répugnant qui n'ignore rien, qui a toujours une réponse prête, la parole mûre sur la branche des lèvres, l'homme qui a étudié les entrailles de la fleur, qui connaît le passé, le présent et le futur, et la généalogie de chaque vague.

Despite all this, the mystery will appear, dressed in its finest garments. The delicate joy of its heaving breasts or the sorrow in its eyes longing only for liberation, need not fear such rivals.

Woman, look into my eyes, these eyes condemned to perpetual chains.

And consider that I could enter God as a diver enters the sea.

But there is no god deep enough for my heart, for the anguish of this heart grown used to the biggest waves and so my heart prefers to vegetate in its harbour, rot amongst the seaweed.

Do not think I am afraid.

Not even a quake shakes me when my eyes open wide and see what can be seen at the moment of death. For I have seen what you will only see then.

I am not afraid.

The only time I shudder is when I encounter my own voice in a man from the past.

—Isolde, watch me in battle, watch me at the most desperate moment, when all is lost. Then, yes, I am truly myself, and I surely look finer than a ship in a death struggle with the sea.

That is what I say, and I prepare to become a root, while the earth flees raging through the heavens, while the moon looks out of the corner of its eye, and the air loses its own boundaries.

What are you doing there, all dressed in black. You stand at the door of my house, awaiting my funeral with wreaths and festive laurels. And what if I order my corpse to be thrown to the dogs?

* * *

Every weight is useless and memory only hinders progress and bends backs. So many arms hang from our necks, and so many breasts and eyes of legendary virgins, that our lips take on the form of obsessed flowers.

Crime is unavoidable if you want to try your wings once more. A gymnast's rhythmic murder or the sleight of hand of a conjurer who knows how to extinguish flames in the womb or shift them at just the right moment, making them appear inside the violin of the most distracted spectator. From there they will climb delicate ladders to the summit of the void.

Malgré tout, le mystère se présentera, vêtu de ses habits de luxe. La joie délicate de ses seins palpitants ou la douleur de ses yeux qui seulement veulent se libérer, ne doivent pas craindre de semblables rivaux.

Femme regarde mes yeux, ces yeux condamnés à la chaîne perpétuelle.

Et pense que je pourrai entrer en dieu comme le scaphandrier dans la mer.

Mais il n'y a pas un dieu suffisamment profond pour mon cœur, pour l'angoisse de ce cœur habitué aux plus grandes vagues et le cœur préfère végéter dans son port et pourrir parmi les algues.

Ne crois pas que j'aie peur.

Pas un tremblement ne me secoue lorsque s'ouvrent grands mes yeux et voient ce que l'on voit au moment de mourir. Parce que j'ai vu ce que vous ne verrez qu'à ce moment-là.

Je n'ai pas peur.

Je tressaille seulement, parfois, lorsque je trouve ma voix dans un homme d'antan.

—Iseult, regarde-moi dans la bataille, regarde-moi dans le moment le plus désespéré quand tout est perdu. Alors oui, je suis moi et sûrement je me vois plus beau qu'un vaisseau luttant à mort contre la mer.

Ainsi je dis et je me prépare à être racine, tandis que la terre fuit mugissant par le ciel, tandis que la lune regarde à la dérobée et l'air perd ses limites propres.

Que faites-vous là, habillé de noir. Vous êtes à la porte de ma maison, attendant mon enterrement avec des couronnes et des lauriers de fête. Et si moi j'ordonne que mon cadavre soit jeté aux chiens?

* * *

Tout poids est inutile et le souvenir uniquement embarrasse la marche et courbe le dos. Tant de bras pendent de notre cou et tant de seins et des yeux des vierges légendaires que nos lèvres prennent forme de fleur obsédée.

Le crime est nécessaire si vous voulez essayer vos ailes une autre fois. Un rythmique assassinat de gymnaste ou le malabarisme du prestidigitateur qui sait éteindre les flammes dans le ventre ou les changer de place à la minute précise en les faisant surgir dans le violon du plus distrait. De là elles monteront en échelles délicates jusqu'au sommet du néant.

Wrapped in bonds of fire, whoever can dance will be chosen and only he will know how to gird the legendary maiden with serpentine coils. There she will remain enchanted until the end of time.

And it would be good if you knew that the weight of the scream will not suffice to break any glowing circles when the grim season arrives and the procession of spectres can be seen all the way to the Pole.

Afterwards comes the festival of mothers and the festival of brides standing atop the tower, their eyes full of intimate rituals, their eyes open so that the four cardinal points can comfortably be born, that they may then grow unrestrained and flood the world.

Ah if only you knew! The soliloquist's hands rise to his brow making a canopy so his eyes might see further.

All this for what? Soon there will be tears, and a death to be chosen from the range selected by the ages.

Do you hear night's coffin being nailed shut? Do you see the naked beauty in her aquarium of death?

The circumference of the sigh where we thought we had buried all the past can become stocked with tropical vegetation and teeming wildlife.

Flowers will grow beneath the aquarium, flowers will grow beneath the cemetery soil and one day the oldest coffin will appear on the ground lifted on the arms of fragrance like sturdy saplings.

—Isolde, the weight of your tears cannot break marble, but behold the miracle wrought by the muscle of memory.

Do you hear night's coffin being nailed shut?

You are the horse that night rides, on its longest journeys.

But you will never reach the end. You will rove across all of mankind's history and will never find what you seek.

The fitness of gravediggers make the world lighter and the spectacle more bearable. We know that rain will last forever on earth, we know that Autumn will be an ever-living source of leaves, an endless cascade amongst the branches. We know that Winter will extend its pole as far as our eyes when fountains turn into statues in the centre of plains whiter than the moon. We know that far away there, at the edge of Winter, the eyes of the woman can be seen who waits in vain, one who forgot that the fault was all hers or should at least have been divided into two equal halves. Winter will take flight, beating its heavy wings of some unknown metal, and that only because you knew how to beg forgiveness.

Enveloppé de lassos de feux celui qui pourrait danser sera le préféré et seulement lui saura entourer la jeune fabuleuse de spirales de serpent. Là elle restera ensorcelée jusqu'à la fin des siècles.

Et il serait bon que vous sachiez que le poids du hurlement ne pourra pas rompre les cercles lumineux lorsque la macabre saison arrivera, et que l'on verra le défilé des spectres vers le pôle.

Après viendra la fête des mères et la fête des fiancées debout sur la tour avec les yeux pleins de cérémonies intimes, les yeux ouverts afin que naissent commodément les quatre points cardinaux qui bientôt croîtront sans mesure et déborderont du monde.

Ah si tu savais! Les mains du soliloque se lèvent jusqu'au front et font auvents aux yeux pour regarder plus loin.

À quoi bon tout cela? Bientôt viendront les larmes et une mort à choisir dans la variété sélectionnée par les siècles.

Entends-tu clouer le cercueil nocturne? Vois-tu la belle nue dans son aquarium de mort?

La circonférence du soupir où nous avons cru inhumer tout ce passé, peut se peupler d'une végétation tropicale et d'une faune vertigineuse.

Des fleurs pousseront sous l'aquarium des fleurs pousseront sous les terres du cimetière, et un jour apparaîtra sur le sol le plus vieux cercueil, levé sur des bras d'odeurs comme des tiges robustes.

—Iseult, le poids des larmes ne peut pas rompre le marbre, mais voilà qui fit le miracle de la mémoire musclée.

Entends-tu clouer le cercueil nocturne?

Tu es le cheval qui monte la nuit, pour ses plus longues marches.

Cependant jamais tu n'arriveras à la fin. Tu parcourras toute l'histoire des hommes et tu ne trouveras pas ce que tu cherchais.

La culture physique des fossoyeurs fait plus léger le monde et plus supportable le spectacle. Nous savons que la pluie de terre sera éternelle, nous savons que l'automne sera une source de feuilles toujours vivante, une cascade interminable parmi les branches. Nous savons que l'hiver allongera son pôle jusqu'à nos yeux quand les jeux d'eau deviennent des statues au milieu des plaines plus blanches que la lune. Nous savons que là-bas, loin, au bord de l'hiver on verra les yeux de celle qui attend en vain et oublia que la faute était sienne ou tout au moins devait se partager en deux moitiés pareilles. L'hiver s'envolera agitant ses ailes lourdes de quelque métal inconnu, et cela uniquement parce que tu sus demander pardon.

On the roads, the legendary caravans will return, possessing no title of nobility but their own antiquity, their obvious experience similar to the pyramids or to the armchair of the mandarin who has heard the music of so many centuries pass by, with no apparent purpose in his eyes, for they were always fixed on the bare breasts of a tortured beauty, writhing upon the infernal bed.

Sometimes before the desired conclusion, the hospital appears, open and tidy in its whiteness, like a restaurant with tables awaiting the equality of feeling.

The unexpected train departs for the satisfaction of its desires. Everywhere there are rifles waiting breathlessly in trembling hands.

Sometimes the ambush comes towards us, sometimes it goes off in other directions, seeming not to have seen us or simply to have forgotten us.

Sometimes thief flees, carrying the severed hand and breasts of the legendary beauty in his pockets; at other times the doctor flees with his bag where he has hidden the eyes of the unforgettable beloved.

The road goes straight on and stops only at the sea. There boats are waiting, leaning against the railings of dusk. At the exact moment of departure the young traveller reappears with her head swathed in seven rainbows, dragging behind her the chorus of supplicants that feed on her sweet breath.

She wants everyone to live preoccupied by her expressive eyes, her neck swathed in melodious lace, her shoulders swathed in magnetic furs and her rainbow-coloured hat.

When she sees our eyes pierced by the light, she is startled; her bones tremble beneath flesh prepared for catastrophe.

All instruments of torture are the same in their innermost raison d'être. Even the doves that fly from sky to sky have known this since their earliest infancy.

The hereditary beauty shackled to her own breasts lives in the innocence of her volatile hair. Never has she looked upon the desperate swallow in its jar of air, nor upon other similar birds, longing to break through the earth's atmosphere and escape our friendship forever.

She bends her head beneath the sky's tattoos and sees nothing. It could scarcely be said she even feels the chains around her womb.

Sur les chemins reviendront les caravanes légendaires qui n'ont pas d'autre titre de noblesse que leur propre ancienneté, leur expérience évidente semblable aux pyramides ou au fauteuil du mandarin qui a entendu passer la musique de tant de siècles sans destin apparent à ses yeux, parce qu'ils étaient toujours fixes dans les seins nus de la belle torturée qui se tord étendue sur les planches infernales.

Parfois avant la fin désirée apparaît l'hôpital ouvert et ordonné dans sa blancheur, comme un restaurant avec ses tables qui attendent l'égalité du sentiment.

Le train inespéré part vers la satisfaction de ses désirs. Partout guette haletant le fusil dans la main tremblante.

Parfois l'embuscade marche vers nous, parfois elle s'éloigne dans d'autres directions et elle semble ne pas nous avoir vus ou bien nous avoir oubliés.

Parfois le voleur fuit emportant la main et les seins coupés de la belle légendaire, dans ses poches, d'autres fois le docteur fuit avec la valise où il a caché les yeux de l'aimée inoubliable.

Le chemin suit droit et s'arrête dans la mer. Là sont les barques attendant appuyées sur la rampe du crépuscule. Au moment du départ définitif apparaît de nouveau la jeune voyageuse avec la tête entourée de sept arcs-en-ciel, traînant à sa suite la chœur des suppliants qui se nourrissent de son haleine précieuse.

Elle veut que tous vivent préoccupés par ses yeux communicants, par son col entouré de dentelles mélodieuses, par ses épaules entourées de fourrures magnétiques et par son chapeau d'arc-en-ciel.

Elle, quand elle voit nos yeux troués par la lumière, s'effraie, ses os tremblent sous la chair préparée aux catastrophes.

Les instruments de torture sont tous semblables par la base interne de leur raison d'être. Même les colombes qui volent de ciel en ciel, savent cela depuis leur plus tendre enfance.

La belle ancestrale enchaînée à ses seins vit dans l'innocence de ses cheveux volatiles. Jamais elle n'a regardé l'hirondelle désespérée dans son bocal d'air ni d'autres oiseaux semblables qui voudraient rompre l'atmosphère terrestre et fuir pour toujours notre amitié.

Elle incline sa tête sous les tatouages du ciel et ne voit rien. À peine on pourrait dire qu'elle sent les chaînes de son ventre.

And do you know why? Because there is never a shortage of dead women cut to pieces by the daggers of the ghost hidden behind these curtains, who in the end makes a gesture of refusal and turns his face away quite naturally.

All brides sleep in the same bed.

There they sleep penetrated by the same dream, their aquatic eyes swimming amongst the same underwater seaweed. Since the beginning of the world the leaves of virginity have fallen outside their own Autumn, for no reason whatsoever.

The lamp that keeps vigil resembles a jellyfish with injured eyes. And they do not understand.

Through the open window the skeleton's hand extends its fingers to lure birds that are irretrievably lost because of their migratory impulses or because of magnets in the forest. And they do not understand.

The birds die, suffocated by their own musical instrument, an instrument whose sound causes our vertebrae to grow and sap to rise to the summit of the brain, feeding the lights at the correct pressure. And they do not understand.

Outside crowds throng together, arguing furiously on the steps of the miraculous sanctuary. On their knees they ascend the stairs of their hymns, attempting to kiss the claws of the twitching dragon.

The captain of the lilies defends the rights of his caste and will continue dispensing perfume as long as he lives and as long as the triumph is his. By contrast the naked woman is struck, and thrown from above, falling and striking her breasts on the steps, where her lamentations shatter.

Thus one day she will fall unexpectedly into the council chamber while the king is in discussions with his favourites. She will be the key to the mystery, because the truth will escape with the blood from her wounds.

There lies the light, light that the monks, concerned only with gathering as much manna as possible and replying to the dragon's greetings, do not care to see.

Blinded by flashes of lightning from the god they worshipped, they froze into statues. This ought to have been their sad end for the sphinx does not return visits, nor does it even open its eyes to witness the cataclysm.

Flee from here. Cross the immense river with a raven on your shoulder, the river that passes like a train and maintains its progress to infinity.

Cross the river that runs between palm trees and storks, palms taller than the eyes of the beloved, the river you do not know, the one I point

Et cela savez-vous pourquoi? Parce qu'il ne manque pas quelque morte déchirée par les poignards du fantôme caché derrière ces rideaux, qui fasse enfin le geste de refuser et de tourner la tête avec naturel.

Toutes les fiancées dorment sur le même lit.

Là elles dorment traversées par le même rêve avec les yeux aquatiques nageants parmi les mêmes algues sous-marines. Depuis le début du monde les feuilles de la virginité tombent hors de leur propre automne, sans aucune raison.

La lampe qui veille est semblable à une méduse aux yeux blessés. Et elles ne comprennent pas.

Par la fenêtre ouverte la main du squelette tend les doigts pour attirer les oiseaux perdus irrémissiblement à cause de leurs élans migrateurs ou des aimants de la forêt. Et elles ne comprennent pas.

Les oiseaux meurent étouffés par leur propre instrument musical, cet instrument au son duquel croissent nos vertèbres et se lève la sève jusqu'au sommet du cerveau pour nourrir les luminaires à la pression due. Et elles ne comprennent pas.

Dehors les foules s'amoncellent et se disputent férocement les marches du sanctuaire miraculeux. Elles montent à genoux par les escaliers de leurs hymnes et essaient d'embrasser les griffes du dragon convulsé.

Le capitaine des lys défend les droits de sa caste et il continuera à parfumer tant qu'il vivra et que le triomphe sera à lui. Par contre la femme nue est frappée et jetée d'en haut, et elle tombe tapant ses seins sur les échelons où se brisent ses plaintes.

Ainsi un jour elle tombera à l'improviste dans la salle du conseil, quand le roi discute avec ses favoris. Elle sera la clé du mystère parce que la vérité s'échappe avec le sang de ses blessures.

Là est la lumière, la lumière que les moines ne voulurent pas voir, préoccupés uniquement à ramasser toute la manne possible et répondre aux saluts du dragon.

Aveuglés par les éclairs du dieu qu'ils adoraient, se figèrent en statues. Ainsi devait être leur triste fin parce que le sphinx ne rend pas les visites et n'ouvre même pas les yeux pour regarder le cataclysme.

Fuis d'ici. Traverse le fleuve immense avec la corneille sur l'épaule, le fleuve qui passe comme un train et suit sa marche jusqu'à l'infini.

Traverse le fleuve qui court entre des palmiers et des cigognes, palmiers plus grands que les yeux de l'aimée, le fleuve que tu ne connais pas, celui

out to you, the one that, at night, fills with magic lanterns, and falls asleep beneath its own canopy, if the impassive shepherdess knows how to sing in its ear.

—Isolde, what is your voice and what should it be? Where is your voice and where should it be?

You will make a harp from the branches and you will scare away the bees. You will be left alone amongst spectres you have lured with your spells. Your delicate fingers will pluck the finest melodies from the trembling leaves and your eyes, up there, will observe the world like the monstrance of emptiness. Do not let the moon undress you, not let yourself be tied to some random star like those hanged men who swing over eternity for beautiful crimes.

What does it matter to you if your suitor throws himself from the tower and loses his sight along the way!

Leave him in peace. You will say that his eyes knew how to die with modest heroism. There will be no lack of those to gather up the voltaic lover's songs, nor of those to light a candle in his memory, or place a menacing wreath upon his skull, where the eyes alone still retain some trace of life, eyes that rise every morning on tiptoe to sow turmoil in your hardened breast.

You sing, oh thoughtless one!, while your snake-like arms writhe like those of Hindu temple dancers.

The waves are slow to die.

Do you hear the sea's coffin being nailed shut?

—Isolde, this other woman also died. He, the guilty man, walks away down the final path, accompanied by his crimes.

They all died. The statues were offloaded at various stops.

With a fixed smile, that woman remained in the middle of the fields. But there is one, there is one that washed up on my memory's sands and who feeds upon my cells.

One day we flew over effervescent peaks. Together we tumbled into the limitless abyss and there we elevated the sorceries of sex to a rite of defenceless shipwreck.

For five months my head slept on her belly. That knot of arteries and bones made our fortune creak from the moment of our luminous encounter. Ever since I have gone on living following her burial.

que je te signale, celui qui, la nuit, se remplit de lanternes magiques et s'endort sous son propre dais, si la bergère impossible sait lui chanter à l'oreille.

—Iseult, quelle est ta voix, et laquelle devrait-elle être? Où est ta voix et où devrait-elle être?

Tu feras une harpe avec les branches, tu effraieras les abeilles. Tu resteras seule au milieu des spectres que tu as su attirer avec tes charmes. Tes doigts délicats arracheront les meilleures mélodies aux feuilles tremblantes et tes yeux là-haut regarderont le monde comme l'ostensoir du vide. Ne permets pas que la lune te déshabille, ni qu'on t'attache à une étoile quelconque comme des pendus pour de beaux délits les pendus qui se bercent au-dessus de l'éternité.

Que t'importe si le galant se jette de la tour et perd la vue en chemin!

Laisse-le en paix. Tu diras que ses yeux surent mourir avec un sobre héroïsme. Il ne manquera pas quelqu'un pour ramasser les chants de l'amant voltaïque, ni quelqu'un pour allumer une bougie en sa mémoire, ou poser une couronne menaçante sur sa tête morte où seuls les yeux gardent encore une certaine vie et se lèvent tous les matins sur la pointe des pieds pour aller semer l'agitation dans ta poitrine endurcie.

Tu chantes, oh inconsciente, tandis qu'agonisent les serpents de tes bras comme les bayadères des temples.

Les vagues sont lentes à mourir.

Entends-tu clouer le cercueil de la mer?

—Iseult, cette autre mourut aussi. Lui le coupable, s'éloigne sur le dernier chemin accompagné de ses crimes.

Toutes moururent. Les statues débarquèrent dans les diverses stations.

Le sourire attaché, celle-là resta au milieu des champs. Mais il y en a une, il y en a une, qui a échoué dans les sables de ma mémoire et se nourrit de mes cellules.

Un jour nous nous envolâmes sur les sommets effervescents. Ensemble nous roulâmes dans l'abîme illimité et là nous élevâmes les sorcelleries du sexe au rite de naufrage sans défense.

Cinq mois ma tête dormit sur son ventre. Ce nœud d'artères et d'os faisait craquer notre fortune après la rencontre lumineuse. Depuis lors je vis en suivant son enterrement.

I go down the stairway of her memory, which every day grows longer and every hour more auspicious, woven with stars that gave her all their light before dying, that bled for her, expecting no reward.

—Isolde, there are times I would like to drown in an ocean of women.

Night reigns on both shores of your gaze and I wander the world, I wander in silence, I wander like the loneliness of a dead man.

I wander through the world without looking at the world, I wander through the world without hearing the world, I wander with the dignity of a dead man.

Do you hear it? They are nailing my coffin shut.

Do you hear how they nail my coffin shut? How they shut the night inside my coffin, the night that will be mine until the end of time?

I am slow to die.

I do not fear the void, nor would I fear it, even if I were not certain of surviving in my echo, surviving intangibly, rolling from echo to echo.

—Isolde, you will encounter me again many times yet, on many roads to eternity.

And some among you will also encounter me, and see my guilty eyes in shackles, struggling to break free.

Watch the dead man rising from the open sea. Listen to the voice of the dead man standing upright amidst his shroud of waves.

Watch the dead man rising on the mountain top.

The great voice of our ancestors, the dark voice whose roots lie in the deepest parts of the earth and take years, centuries, to reach the surface, and still more years and more centuries to find a throat that is ready for it.

A throat powerful enough to be like a trumpet. The trumpet of the ages, the trumpet of all who have suffered, of all who have trembled and sweated blood in terror and exhaustion, the trumpet of all sorrows, the trumpet of all rancour, all vengeance. The trumpet with terrifying roots.

Listen, listen to the voice of darkness. Through my throat the darkness returns to light.

Enter your own dizzying cavern, descend without chloroform to your innermost depths. Blood has its own light and bones spark with fevered phosphorous, like an electrical contact.

Je vais descendant l'escalier de son souvenir qui chaque jour devient plus long et chaque heure plus propice, entretissé par des étoiles qui lui donnèrent toute sa lumière avant de mourir, qui se saignèrent pour elle, sans attendre aucune récompense.

—Iseult, parfois je voudrais me noyer dans un océan de femmes.

Règne la nuit sur les deux rives de ton regard et je me promène par le monde, je me promène en silence, je me promène semblable à la solitude d'un mort.

Je me promène par le monde sans regarder le monde, je me promène par le monde sans entendre le monde, je me promène semblable à la dignité d'un mort.

Entends-tu? On est en train de clouer mon cercueil.

Entends-tu comme on cloue mon cercueil? Comme on enferme la nuit dans mon cercueil, la nuit qui sera mienne jusqu'à la fin des siècles?

Je suis lent à mourir.

Je ne crains pas le néant et ne le craindrais pas même si je n'étais sûr de continuer dans mon écho, de continuer intangible, roulant d'écho en écho.

—Iseult, tu me rencontreras encore plusieurs fois sur plusieurs chemins de l'éternité.

Et aussi quelques-uns parmi vous me rencontreront, et verront mes yeux coupables attachés par des menottes et se débattant pour les briser.

Regardez le mort qui se lève dans la haute mer. Écoutez la voix du mort qui se dresse au milieu de son suaire de vagues.

Regardez le mort qui se lève sur le sommet de la montagne.

La grande voix des aïeux, la voix noire qui a sa racine au plus profond de la terre, et qui met des années et des siècles pour arriver à la surface, et plus d'années et plus de siècles à trouver une gorge préparée.

La gorge puissante qui soit comme une trompette. La trompette des âges, la trompette de tous ceux qui ont souffert, de tous ceux qui ont tremblé en sueur de sang sur la terreur ou la défaillance, la trompette de toutes les douleurs, de toutes les rancunes, de toutes les vengeances. La trompette aux racines effrayantes.

Écoutez, écoutez la voix des ténèbres. Par ma gorge les ténèbres reviennent à la lumière.

Entrez dans votre propre caverne vertigineuse, descendez sans chloroforme dans vos intimes profondeurs. Le sang a sa lumière propre et les os jettent des étincelles à cause d'un phosphore fiévreux semblable a un contact électrique.

Ladies and Gentlemen: There is a dead man inside his coffin flattening the hair beneath his head. You have fine teeth for uttering fine words.

Ladies and Gentlemen: There is a bird opening up in full flight and hurling eternity at us. Hurling it at us along with its blood and viscera like excrement.

The bird prophesied by inexorable astronomers knows all secrets.

Ladies and Gentlemen: there is a dead man in his coffin, turning into a skeleton. The emanations from his flesh split the wood and make the stone doors shake.

You have heard the tomb's doors creaking and thought that, two metres below, there lay a city of quiet skeletons and bare-toothed skulls. There is a city of waxen faces and waxen hands. The age-old dust from your bones thickens the nights, falling like time into your inner water-clock because your shadow takes the form of night and it is a little night in motion.

You are there in that endless position where you have remained since drinking the glass of infinity which distils the void and turns you into the respectable ash of an immemorial ancestor. Out of all these ashes chance may forge a new star.

And I tell you, dear listeners, that the unfortunate skeleton that is your host will never see the light, for he will pass from the coffin of your flesh to the coffin of the tomb. Thus you carry a shackled prisoner into your pitiless drifter's dungeon. It is bad luck to be carried on this framework that will take its revenge one day, and is looking for the right moment.

The prisoner thirsts for warmth like an excited sister, feels a heavenly delirium in his heart, wants to escape this endless evening, leap forth with a wild croak, like the volcano erupting from the bowels of the earth, not stopping until it reaches the light, as the prophesied terror bursts from his chest and rises to his lips and to his eyes, which turn into wounds of silence. Your bones, drunk on solitude, sense the murmuring dew in the blood and suspect they are the final music, the dying hiss after the end of the world, comparable only to the siren of a wrecked ship suddenly resounding on the sea floor.

And, Ladies and Gentlemen, when the bones break the ties that bind them like constellations, there will be a fabulous noise, a noise catastrophic for sensitive ears, more violent than the noise of distant things breaking free and galloping away. Such is the anxiety of the escaped prisoner, who

Mesdames et Messieurs: Il y a un mort qui aplatit ses cheveux sous la tête dans son cercueil. Vous avez de belles dents pour dire de belles paroles.

Mesdames et Messieurs: Il y a un oiseau qui s'ouvre en plein vol et nous jette l'éternité. Nous jette avec son sang et ses viscères l'éternité comme un excrément.

L'oiseau deviné par les astronomes inexorables connaît tous les secrets.

Mesdames et Messieurs: Il y a un mort qui devient squelette dans son cercueil. Les émanations de la chair fendent le bois et font osciller les portes de pierre.

Vous avez entendu craquer les portes du tombeau et vous avez pensé que, à deux mètres de profondeur il y a une ville de squelettes placides et des crânes mordeurs. Il y a une ville de faces de cire et des mains de cire. La poussière séculaire de vos os endurcit les nuits et tombe comme le temps dans votre clepsydre interne parce que votre ombre a la forme de la nuit et qu'elle est une petite nuit en marche.

Vous êtes là dans cette interminable position dans laquelle vous restez après avoir bu le verre d'infini qui distille le vide et qui vous convertit en cendre respectable d'ancêtre immémorial. De toutes ces cendres le hasard peut faire un astre nouveau.

Et je vous dis, chers auditeurs, que le squelette malheureux qui est votre hôte, jamais ne verra la lumière, car il passera du cercueil de votre chair au cercueil du tombeau. Ainsi vous portez un prisonnier attaché dans votre cachot vagabond et sans pitié. Mauvaise fortune est celle d'aller au dos de cette armature qui doit se venger et qui guette le moment favorable.

Le prisonnier a soif de température comme la sœur ardente, il sent des délires de ciel dans ses entrailles, il veut sortir de ce soir constant, sauter dans un croassement sauvage comme le volcan saute au fond de la terre et ne s'arrête avant d'arriver à la lumière, comme l'effroi divinatoire jaillit de la poitrine et monte jusqu'aux lèvres et jusqu'aux yeux convertis en plaies de silence. Vos os ivres de solitude sentent les rumeurs de la rosée dans le sang et devinent qu'ils sont la dernière musique, le dernier sifflement après la fin du monde, seul semblable à la sirène d'un bateau naufragé qui retentirait soudain au fond de la mer.

Et quand les os, Mesdames et Messieurs, rompront les lacets qui les lient entre eux comme les constellations, ils feront un bruit fabuleux, un bruit de catastrophe, pour les oreilles accordées, plus violent que celui des lointains qui se libèrent et s'éloignent au galop. Telle est l'anxiété du

makes the roads howl and who startles gutless time, a time that mimics the gestures of the universe.

Ladies and Gentlemen, the viper from the shipwrecks bites its own tail and grows, grows, expanding into infinity. We are there within its coils, sucked into the abyss of impending decay, our eyes oozing pus like spume upon the shore. Meanwhile the landscapes within us sense the flight of trees; our ears, before coming off and falling like leaves, manage to hear the whirlwind of sinking wheat fields. There is no hope of rest. In vain the skeleton behind the window strikes the hieratic pose of one about to sing. The planet's inner doors violently cover their ears, like the nurse who cannot bear the clamour from the terrible adventure at the final frontier. Nothing is gained by thinking that the voluptuous realm of wonder stretches beyond the abstract wall.

No, you will not find the old man sitting on the rocks of eternal snow, smiling softly and surrounded by meditative heroes like palm trees.

A couple of words more, my friends, before I finish: our struggles and our arguments are in vain, our phosphorescing blades and words are in vain. Only the coffin is correct. Victory belongs to the cemetery. Only in the mysterious furrow can triumph flourish.

Such was the speech that, for no reason, you called grim, the beautiful speech of the presenter of the void.

Go on. Follow your path as I follow mine.

I am too slow in dying.

Nevertheless, Isolde, prepare your tears. Distant, softened, like a piano of remorse, prepare your finest tears.

I am slow to die.

The statue wanders over the sea and the wind closes my eyelids in a sign of penetrating glory.

A mountain takes up half my chest.

I have too big a heart for you. You have measured your mountains, you know that Gaurishankar is 8,800 metres high, but you will never know the elevation of my heart. Yet, tomorrow, from deep within the earth I will hear your footsteps.

Who will disturb the peace? Silence this insolent noise.

Those are my ancestors dancing on my tomb. Those are my forebears tolling the bell to wake me.

prisonnier évadé qui fait hurler les chemins et qui épouvante le temps sans entrailles, le temps qui fait des gestes d'univers.

Mesdames et Messieurs, la couleuvre des naufrages se mord la queue et s'agrandit, s'agrandit jusqu'à l'infini. Nous sommes là en dedans de ses cercles, aspirés par l'abîme de la future pourriture, rendant du pus par nos yeux comme écume de plages. En même temps les paysages internes sentent l'envol des arbres, nos oreilles avant de se décoller et de tomber comme des feuilles, parviennent à entendre le tourbillon des épis qui s'approfondissent. Il n'y a pas d'espoir de repos. En vain le squelette derrière sa vitre prend l'attitude hiératique de celui qui va chanter. Les portes internes de la planète se couvrent les oreilles avec violence comme l'infirmier qui entend les clameurs de la terrible aventure à l'ultime frontière. On ne gagne rien à penser que peut-être derrière la muraille abstraite s'étend la zone voluptueuse de l'étonnement.

Non, vous ne trouverez pas le vieillard assis sur les roches de la neige éternelle, souriant sans dureté et entouré de héros méditatifs comme des palmiers.

Deux mots encore, chers amis, avant de terminer: vaines sont nos luttes et nos discussions, vaine la phosphorescence de nos épées et de nos paroles. Seul le cercueil a raison. La victoire appartient au cimetière. Le triomphe fleurit seulement dans le sillon mystérieux.

Tel fut le discours que vous avez appelé macabre sans aucune raison, le beau discours du présenteur du néant.

Passez. Suivez votre chemin comme je suis le mien.

Je suis trop lent à mourir.

Cependant Iseult prépare tes larmes. Lointaine attendrie comme un piano de remords, prépare tes meilleures larmes.

Je suis lent à mourir.

La statue se promène sur la mer et le vent ferme mes paupières en signe de gloire pénétrante.

Une montagne occupe la moitié de ma poitrine.

Je porte un cœur trop grand pour vous. Vous avez mesuré vos montagnes, vous savez que le Gaurizankar a huit mille huit cents mètres de hauteur, mais vous ne saurez jamais la hauteur de mon cœur. Pourtant demain du fond de la terre j'écouterai vos pas.

Qui troublera le silence? Apaisez ce bruit insolent.

Ce sont mes ancêtres qui dansent sur ma tombe. Ce sont mes aïeux qui sonnent le tocsin pour me réveiller.

It is the leader of the tribe, standing alone and weeping.

Hush your useless cries.

Here we are at last, asleep in the earth's vulva.

Since then the cataclysm abides in the cities. Walls fall and roofs too, revealing entire peoples naked in various poses, most of the time begging for mercy.

Arms and legs can be seen amongst the rubble.

And then even the sky caved in. How many birds perished, crushed.

For days afterwards crowds wandered past, looking at the ruins. Not even a smile was left standing. Ghosts walked past with their eyes open, howling, and a crazed man leaped headlong, dagger in hand, looking for a guilty god.

Sweat, slaves, raise up the cities of the future. Meanwhile I watch the progress of the forests. I reflect on the pirate of dusk, and his slow torment.

Measure the earth to learn how many miracles it can hold. Adorn the volcanoes, decorate the rivers, tunnel through mountains. You can tell me tomorrow how many ghosts might yet be buried along with all their dreams.

Awake, Isolde, before the final uprising comes, and your bed is riddled with bullets because no-one believes in your truth.

I tell you, it will be your grace that has to rise amidst the corpses, your grace caught in the wheels of the riot, while fire consumes all and begins licking at the horizon, climbing into the sky. Towers give way under the incessant rain. Flaming roofs fly by.

All things must pass. From end to end the world is in silence. But there is still something searching for us everywhere.

Plough the earth and sow wonders. Throw ladders into every abyss.

Tell me, what use is hope? Sailing ships move away to their endless Golgotha, for fear of the storm. Behind them, everything remains.

The canoe that ought to perish is already cresting the final wave.

The sky is slow to die.

Do you hear the sky's coffin being nailed shut?

C'est le chef de la tribu qui se trouve seul et qui pleure.

Apaisez vos cris inutiles.

Nous voici enfin endormis dans le sexe de la terre.

Depuis lors le cataclysme vit dans les villes. Les murs tombent et les toits, laissant voir des peuples entiers nus en diverses attitudes, la plupart des fois en implorant miséricorde.

On voit des bras et des jambes parmi les décombres.

Il y eut aussi alors un écroulement dans le ciel. Combien d'oiseaux moururent écrasés.

Les jours après les foules se promenaient en regardant les ruines. Il ne resta pas un sourire debout. Les fantômes passaient hurlant avec les yeux ouverts, et un homme affolé sautait de tête en tête un poignard à la main cherchant un dieu coupable.

Suez, esclaves, levez les villes futures. Moi pendant ce temps je regarde la course des forêts. Je contemple le pirate du couchant et son lent supplice.

Mesurez la terre pour savoir combien de miracles peuvent y tenir. Ornez les volcans, pavoisez les rivières, creusez les montagnes. Vous me direz demain combien de fantômes on peut enterrer encore avec tous leurs rêves.

Réveille-toi, Iseult, avant qu'arrive la révolte finale et que ton lit soit criblé de balles, parce que personne ne croit à ta vérité.

Il faudra, je te dis, que ta grâce se lève au milieu des cadavres, ta grâce prise dans les roues de l'émeute tandis que le feu détruit tout et commence à lécher l'horizon et à grimper par le ciel. Les tours s'affaissent sous la pluie illimitée. Des toits en flammes volent.

Tout doit passer. De bord à bord le monde est en silence. Mais il y a quelque chose qui nous cherche encore partout.

Labourez la terre pour semer des prodiges. Jetez des échelles dans tous les abîmes.

Dîtes-moi quelle utilité présente l'espérance? Les voiliers s'éloignent sur leur Golgotha interminable par crainte de la bourrasque. Derrière tout reste.

Le canot qui doit périr monte déjà la dernière vague.

Le ciel est lent à mourir.

Entends-tu clouer le cercueil du ciel?

Notes

General note:
Given the nature of the text, the author's cultural background, and the fact he had already made extensive correlations between his personal situation with Ximena and that of Christ and the Passion in the poem, 'Pasión, Pasión y Muerte' (Passion, Passion and Death, 1926), it will be no surprise that there are a number of biblical references throughout the poem. I do not believe that these need to be itemised, as they will be obvious to those who are able to spot them, and irrelevant, even tedious, to those who are unable to. They add to the overall feel of the work, to its somewhat blasphemous mood and to its oracular tone.

p.14/15; p.72/73 *Destruirlo todo, todo, a bala y a cuchillo / Destroy all of it, all of it, with bullet and blade / Il faut tout détruire, tout…*
    Probably a nod towards the exhortation to gratuitous deeds in André Breton's *First Surrealist Manifesto*.

p.16/17; p.74/75 *La calle de los sueños tiene un ombligo… / The street of dreams has an enormous navel… / La rue des rêves a un nombril immense…*
    Cedomil Goic (in the *Obra poética*, 2003) claims that the imagery owes something to the paintings of *Navels and Bottles* by Hans (Jean) Arp. Given the close connection between the two men, this is quite possible.

—*Los cantores cardíacos mueren sólo de pensar en ello / Faint-hearted singers die at the very thought of it / Les chanteurs cardiaques meurent à cette seule pensée*
    As René de Costa has pointed out, this almost certainly refers to the legends that surround the part of Tristan in Wagner's opera—one of the most strenuous tenor roles in the repertory—following the death of Ludwig Schnorr von Carolsfeld, its first interpreter, after only four performances. Two conductors have subsequently died while conducting the opera.

p.18/19; p.76/77 *Había entonces un desfile de marineros ante un rey / Then there was a procession of sailors before a king / Il y avait un défilé de matelots devant un roi…*
    René de Costa believes that this refers to a production of *Tristan and Isolde* seen by Huidobro in Paris in 1928.

p.20/21; p.78/79 *Que pase corriendo el asesino disparando balazos sin control a sus perseguidores / Let the killer run past, firing wild shots at his pursuers / Que l'assassin passe en courant et tirant*

It is tempting to see this a coy allusion to the author's elopement with Ximena, during the course of which it was said that he fired a pistol at her pursuing family's car, or at least at its tyres. The famous photo by Hans Arp of the pistol-wielding Huidobro (to be seen on the back cover of this book) is likewise almost certainly such an allusion. It is quite possible that there was no truth to the story at all, but Huidobro did like to tell stories where he was the hero.

p.34/35; 92/93 — *Al criminal etc. / Get the criminal etc / À l'assassin etc. / Get the killer… etc.*, & *A la guillotina / À la guillotine! / To the guillotine! etc.*

This section sounds oddly like one of the stories in *Tres inmensas novelas*, by *Huidobro and Hans Arp*, in this case 'El Gato con botas' (Puss in Boots), a story actually written by Huidobro alone to pad out what would otherwise have been too short a book for his Chilean publisher. See p.78-79 of our edition of *Three Huge Novels* (Shearsman Books, 2020), translated by Tony Frazer. *Skyquake* pre-dates the story by a good five years or so.

p.60/61; p.118/119 —*Isolda, aquella otra también murió. El, el culpable, se aleja por el último camino acompañado de sus crímenes. / —Isolde, that other woman also died. He, the guilty one, departs on his final path accompanied by his crimes. / Iseult, cette autre mourut aussi…*

and:

Final paragraphs: *Un día volamos enlazados sobre las cimas efervescentes. […] sin esperar recompensa alguna. / One day we flew bound together over effervescent peaks. […] expecting no reward. / Un jour nous nous envolâmes sur les sommets effervescents…*

Cedomil Goic sees these lines—correctly, I think—as an allusion to Teresa Wilms Montt (1893–1921), the tragic young Chilean writer whom VH had assisted in 1916 in her escape to Argentina from the convent in which her irate husband had immured her. This event, and their subsequent brief affair, is a clear foreshadowing of VH's later "abduction" of Ximena, and this part of the text suggests a similar sexual obsession. [The work of Teresa Wilms Montt is finally being made available, albeit mostly in Spanish at this stage, and is worth exploring. —*TF.*] It may of course refer

only to the escape with Ximena, but, given the way VH typically layers his work, I think it unlikely.

p.66/67; p.124/125 *Henos al fin dormidos en el carne de la tierra / Here we are at last sleeping in the earth's flesh / Nous voici enfin endormis dans le sexe de la terre*

Here 'carne' (*flesh*) replaces the word 'sexo' (*sex*, or in this translation, *vulva*) from the first Madrid edition. The French version retains the original wording. The revision seems to me to be an improvement in both languages.

www.ingramcontent.com/pod-product-compliance
Lightning Source LLC
Chambersburg PA
CBHW031347160426
43196CB00007B/755